WHAT OTHERS ARE

CAN YOU SEE ME NOW?

I'm so excited for you to read Cheri's book! Although I could share what a wise and insightful writer she is based on her Bible plans' excellent reach and performance in our Bible App, honestly the part I'm most excited about sharing is how Cheri lives as a mother, wife, and Jesus-follower. She and her husband Chad practically live out the gospel in a way that is indeed good news for the lonely, left out, and less than. You know what it's like when you see someone access God's grace and exercise His compassion at a level that you just know isn't humanly possible? I get that same earthly glimpse of Jesus when I talk to her or watch her in action with her beautiful family, so you'll surely see it come through the pages of this book.

~Kendra Golden, Head of Content, YouVersion Bible App

We women too often struggle to feel needed and wanted. We search for purpose because we long for our lives to have significance. In her new book, Cheri Strange points us to the One who provides all that and more! Cheri shows us how to experience joy and fulfillment by finding our worth in God and living out His purposes for our lives.

~Kathy Howard, Bible teacher and author of twelve books including *Heirloom: Living & Leaving a Legacy of Faith* and the *Deep Rooted* devotional series.

Cheri takes us on an honest, personal, and vulnerable journey from living in the shadows feeling forgotten and invisible to living a life with value and purpose; being seen, heard, and known while falling in love with God. Such a compelling and encouraging read for all women and teen girls.

~Angela Haynes, pastor's wife and co-author with Brian Haynes of *Relentless Parenting*.

This book is a must-read. Packed with personal anecdotes and based on biblical truth, its daily readings and personal plan for becoming invincible lead readers into the freedom their souls crave. Say goodbye to your wallflower existence and embrace God's unique and power-packed purpose for your life.

~Grace Fox, international speaker, podcaster, and author of *Moving from Fear to Freedom: A Woman's Guide to Peace in Every Situation*

Cheri Strange articulates the hidden thoughts of millions of women who feel unseen, unappreciated, and unwanted. Does God see me? Does He care? With courage and transparency, she invites us along on a 90-day journey to vibrancy and invincibility. She shows us the way to spiritual health and biblical thinking while empowering us to live life God created us to live.

–Lori Hatcher, author of *Refresh Your Prayers, Uncommon Devotions to Restore Power and Praise*

Cheri Strange has impacted generations of our people through her teaching. I continually place her before our students, because she teaches Scripture with wisdom and high responsibility. She is careful and faithful. Listen. Learn. Apply.

–Kade Pierce, Pastor of Students and Missions, Bay Area Church

Can You See Me Now? will bless you as you unpack practical truths from deep insights each and every day that you read. Cheri Strange is a trusted teacher and friend who digs deeply into the gospel truths that she enjoys. Paul once wrote to the Ephesians: "For we are his workmanship, created in Christ Jesus for good works, which God prepared beforehand, that we should walk in them"(Ephesians 2:10). Cheri is deeply committed to helping others know they are well-crafted displays of God's majesty and grace. Her writing is inspiring, practical, and full of insights that help others pursue their life with excellence, in grace, for the glory of God. My wife and I have benefited from her friendship and her steady example of a Christ-centered motherhood and marriage. May God help you discover something beautiful about who He made you to be and what awaits your tomorrow. I truly believe *Can You See Me?* Now will help each reader toward this end.

–Jason Goings, Grace Baptist Church, Pastor of Preaching and Vision

CHERI STRANGE

can you see me now?

GOOD NEWS FOR THE LONELY,
LEFT OUT, & LESS THAN

CAN YOU SEE ME NOW?

GOOD NEWS FOR THE LONELY, LEFT OUT, AND LESS THAN

CHERI STRANGE

Bold Vision Books
PO Box 2011
Friendswood, Tx 77549

Copyright ©Cheri Strange 2022

ISBN 978-1-946708-762
Library of Congress Control Number 2022943998

All rights reserved.
Published by Bold Vision Books, PO Box 2011, Friendswood, Texas 77549
www.boldvisionbooks.com

Cover Art by Amber Wiegand-Buckley
Cover Design by Barefoot Creative Media
Interior design by kae Creative Solutions

Published in the United States of America.

DEDICATION

To

Taylor, Addison, Jolee, Sophia, Zoe, and Chloe

May you never settle for anything less than
the zebra you were created to become.

TABLE OF CONTENTS

PART II

PART III

PART IV

CHAPTER 7: HOW TO BECOME VIBRANT /177

PART V

CHAPTER 8: HOW TO BECOME INVINCIBLE /204

INTRODUCTION

NO LONGER INVISIBLE

Maybe it's just me. Maybe I'm just not good enough
to get to know. Maybe I'm just not the most fun or
outgoing. Maybe I'm just not likable. No matter what I
do, I'm just tired of feeling invisible.

~Cheyenne[1]

If you have ever felt left out of the group, you just found your
tribe. If your friends and colleagues ignore you in conversations,
or people pass you over, look no further. There is solace here. But let's
get real. It's more than a few isolated incidents of being overlooked,
isn't it? You know the emptiness of never being missed. Your world is
passing you by without inviting you to come along. Maybe you have
even felt the humiliation of being—or at least wondering whether
you might be—replaceable. A mere fixture. Unnoticed. Invisible. All
these ponderings and experiences are fresh reminders which grieve
mercilessly that what you bring to the table is not relevant. You are
not important.

These experiences of being forgotten, left out, completely alone,
and unseen, as if no one knows you well, are more universal than you
might think.[2] But few of us approach the issue in a life-changing way.
Instead, we deal with our pain in the short term, like putting on a
pretty new t-shirt.

The new t-shirt, even one with a God-honoring message, will not
alter my life or yours in any significant way beyond maybe improving
our mood for the day. Although I am for sporting the God-honoring
visual, the visual is rarely life-changing. Something more is needed.

Deep down, we know this.

We know this like we know every good Christian should spend time alone with Jesus in prayer and reading her Bible every day. An age-old message, I know. Yet a large percentage of us simply don't comply. We might pray. Perhaps we fit it in while driving. Squeeze in five-minutes with God or, for the gold star, sign up with a favorite Christian app for the "verse of the day" so we have something spiritual to post on our social media profiles. With a pretty background. Because visuals.

These reminders and attempts are all good and encouraging. I'm all for each one. I even write some of this positive vibe stuff myself. To be honest, it's not life-changing. It has the same effect as wearing Scripture on a pretty t-shirt. While these avenues serve their purposes, I'm fooling no one into believing sporting a God-honoring t-shirt makes me godly, any more than posting a Bible verse of the day. Wearing a shirt is not transformational. It's simply cute.

And this, my friend, is why you are here.

You are looking for more than a God-vibe aesthetic to remedy the hurt within.

I know because it's where I found myself on a similar day. I, too, recognized my need for a remedy. Cute t-shirts were no longer fooling anyone, especially my new husband. I understood early in my married life the handsome man sharing the toothpaste believed he married a *good Christian girl*. My shortcomings in this arena sent me further into the deep recesses of the sidelines. Here I sat in all my inconsistency with the Lord, trying to hide my issues under God-honoring t-shirts and cuteness in front of the Bible-major pastor I married. My efforts were as effective as you can imagine. Cunning shenanigans fooled no one. My t-shirt cover-up was a farce.

In all the cuteness I could muster, I took my inconsistent self on a quest to find a solution, which landed me at our Christian bookstore. Fifteen minutes later, I had my solution. I purchased a One Year Bible. Across 365 days, in about fifteen-minute increments, I could cover the entire book. There were starting and stopping points marked. All for the same price of a t-shirt, pretty or otherwise. Perfect. No more inconsistency. No more hiding on the side, afraid someone will discover my lack. I was on my way to becoming the girl I wanted to become.

I'd like to say I left my inconsistency and shortcomings behind, but I cannot. Failure ensued almost immediately and continued for close to a decade. Seems I'm comfortable sporting an inspirational appearance that runs no deeper than the cotton blend surface. Nine straight years, I fell short of achieving the goal. In many aspects, I continued to sustain life by clinging to aesthetics rather than substance. It was not every word, every day with Jesus, in 365 days a year. But it was truly transformational.

My single bookstore decision started me on a life-changing trajectory. And we will get to how it all fits together to influence your life in the coming pages. What I really want to know is where you find yourself today. Are you weary of your efforts to be seen while settling for cuteness? Do you long to leave the loneliness you feel from being overlooked? Is your desire to be deeply known and loved? Are you ready to reject those wallflower notions that you are less than, or better off left on the periphery? Do you want genuine transformation? If so, this is the place for you. By the time you finish this book, I pray God will equip you with the tools, resources, and knowledge you need to leave shadow living to move toward becoming seen.

But you can't go like that. You need a plan. True and lasting transformation sounds good and hope-filled, but it's never going to happen if you approach it willy-nilly. God never intended you to feel worthless and overlooked. His will is not for you to shrink back and disappear. For your good, He provided a roadmap to enable you to be seen in your personality and beauty. Not in the forced and obnoxious way. Not like the girl across the room with the purposefully exaggerated laugh, perfected for turning heads and stopping all activity in her surrounding spaces. Off-putting and unsavory stage mastering are not in the plan. Neither are we after attention-grabbing avenues like vying for the spotlight with our outfits, tattoos, and hair color. Wear it, tat it, color it if you love it, but our purpose here is not to use aesthetic devices as the mechanism for being noticed when you are weary of blending into the curtains.

You have authentic God-given standout potential without all the paraphernalia. What you need is a plan of biblical proportions to become conspicuous for all the right reasons in all the right ways, and this book offers one with support and guidance. In the back of this book, you will find "My Personal Plan for Becoming Invincible." This is your roadmap for how to experience life seen, known, and loved regardless of your circumstances. May God use this tool, your time, and His Word to take you on a journey from this day forward in which you will soon declare with your life, *I am no longer invisible.*

PART I
CHAPTER 1

WALLFLOWER DAYS

How do you move from living in the shadows, feeling like you have been left behind, to living seen, loved, known, even cherished, if nothing around you makes a shift in that direction?

Good question. It's one I could not get past or articulate in so many words at the time. But today I'm living on the other side of this question. I know now what I didn't know then. You can see me now, where I would have stood camouflaged before. Today, I am secure in who God is making me to be and that is not holding up a wall somewhere in obscurity. No longer am I invisible.

My friend, the same can happen for you. This is not a self-help book. I will not be offering a path toward fame, showing you the ropes for making a name for yourself in order to be taken seriously. But change is possible.

This is a tale of one wallflower nobody and how she became invincible. Allow me to invite you into my story. I believe it will prove significant for you in yours.

Day 1:
Wallflowers Unite

Wallflower: (wawl-flou-er) 1. A person who, because of shyness, unpopularity, or lack of a partner, remains at the side at a party or dance; 2. Any person that remains on or has been forced to the sidelines of any activity.[3]

Call me a wallflower. Unequivocally. A natural observer. Shy. Small. Quiet. The person on the side. Never the girl center-stage with all eyes on her. Not a chance. Glued to the railing, desk, brick, or whatever fixture was the furthest available to keep me from the majority—that's where you would find me in my childhood, when everything was as it should be.

Naturally, you can imagine the response a wallflower has when the stars do not align, trouble erupts, and life gets messy. Wallflowers retract. Already timid, I found more ways to blend into my surroundings. My less than perfect reality wasn't something I shared with people. Developmentally, during the stages a girl typically learns security, when she should be a delight, wanted, and seen, insecurity ran amuck within me. I figured I was a problem better left in the shadows.

God seemed to agree with my limited understanding. Oh, I was a card-carrying believer in Jesus. He had taken away my sin, forgiven all wrongdoing, and destined me for heaven when I died. But He was watching over me like a chaperone at the prom. Somehow, I latched onto believing God loved me and cared for me from afar, like the song "Jesus Loves the Little Children."

Jesus loves the little children,

All the children of the world.

Red and yellow, black and white.

All are precious in His sight.

Jesus loves the little children of the world.[4]

Yes. He loved me. God loved me along with all the other children of the world, as a member of humanity, but not specifically. He didn't love me as a person, with quirky favorites like tater tots and cinnamon candy. It's as if He invited me along with all the girls in my class to the prom. The God of the universe wanted me to be there for the big event, but didn't care about my dress or if anyone ever asked me to dance. I could fade into the themed decorations, unnoticed.

Maybe you can relate. Your proneness to a wallflower mentality may result from some emotional neglect from your childhood. Psychologists suggest some people feel the impact of what did *not* occur in their upbringings long into adulthood. A person could have experienced a happy childhood, absent of trauma, yet had vital emotional needs remain unmet.[5] Your reality may reflect those prior years because individuals who encounter this phenomenon of childhood emotional neglect often shrink back and hang on the sidelines as adults.[6]

Could it be an overarching feeling of isolation? Maybe you feel as if no one really knows you? Do you feel alone in your interests? Is there a pervading sense people are not really with you? Well, Sister, you are in good company. More than half the American population feels the same way.[7]

Many of us feel alone, as if the bulk of our relationships are meaningless. Add some misguided theological underpinnings, all the misfortunes compounding insecurities through adolescence, and you've got the makings of a bona fide wallflower. The good news is, even though you feel like a wallflower, you do not need to remain one.

19

... fear not, for I am with you; be not dismayed, for I am your God; I will strengthen you, I will help you, I will uphold you with my righteous right hand.

Isaiah 41:10 ESV

GOODBYE WALLFLOWER WAYS—

Write this prayer in a notebook or pen one of your own.

God, help me understand why I feel so alone and isolated. Help me trust You will be faithful to strengthen me and hold me until I no longer feel invisible.

Day 2:
The Big Cover Up

The past gets carried with us. It's always there.

~Ann Pearlman[8]

I'm not sure what you do with your junk, but I keep mine pretty handy, somewhere easily accessible. I hauled all of my isolation, acquired insecurity, and bad theology to college. When college ended, I threw my carefully preserved bucket of badness into a suitcase and signed a marriage license with Mr. Perfect. This guy was nothing like me. He was most definitely visible. Mr. Perfect was president of this and that, top all-around guy with the medals and accolades to prove it, highly esteemed by most, and a preacher to boot.

Marrying Mr. Perfect did nothing for my status, but it called into question *his* judgment. Between the two of us, there was a glaring disparity. Often it was obvious. Too many times, it was hurtful. Within a few years, the chasm grew. Not only was my man able to pastor a church, he was wicked smart in the sciences. By the end of my Master's program, Chad was accepted to medical school. As we moved into his medical school years, I, the non-medical-doctor-to-be, ceased to exist.

There was no competing. The lines are announced and drawn for you by those around you. I'm not saying I wanted to compete for the limelight or be "as good as." No, but it would have been nice to be recognized as a person who had value.

My life was neither interesting nor exciting. At least, it wasn't as exciting as the doctor-to-be. Few inquired about it. Many ignored me completely. From our church, to family, to our social connections, the value of my existence was attributed to my relationship to my spouse. I discerned it was best to stick to the sidelines and pipe down. Our friends and family weren't there to hang with me, anyway. I was a subtle piece of the Mr. Perfect package. Blending into the wallpaper was where I belonged.

For years I lived the American Dream, something many people angle and fandangle for. Some dream. I was hollow on the inside, inconspicuous to the world, and miserable with the person I was.

Could my problem be pride? Jealousy? Loneliness? I will admit, there was likely a mixture of those elements. Of all the aspirations I held for my life, none of them included becoming a mere fixture. Purely functional. Overlooked. Insignificant. Replaceable. Or completely invisible. What do you do when you know you are living out the decisions God has led you to make, but they are killing you on the inside?

My reality all those years confirmed what I painstakingly bundled in the suitcase, including my theology: God loved me with an obligatory *bless her heart*, kind of love. I am one of the many children of the world He's willing to save, but not one He desires to use. I am invited to the prom, but my place is on the wall. No pictures. No dancing. God reserved intimacy for big shots like my spouse and his friends. It was not for wallflower nobodies—timid, comfortable in the shadows, less-thans—like me.

Mine was a private and internal struggle. I mean, how do you express to someone what is going on? You are not sure anything is *wrong*. You reason with yourself, *You are probably just jealous.* The problem boils down to the same denominator: you. Time and time again. Situation after situation. The fault must lie with me. Changing locations will not matter. Starting over at a new job, with different friends, with a new church, doesn't help. You alone know there is an emptiness, and it is not going away.

Maybe you possess your own suitcase bulging with hurts, disappointments, and misgivings for what you thought your life should've been. Maybe you are not living your idea of the American Dream—or any dream for that matter.

If you have ever thought yourself to be nothing more than a fixture or reduced The Problem to, well . . . *you*, help is here.

> *O people in Zion who dwell in Jerusalem, you will weep no more. The LORD will be gracious to you when you cry out to him for help; when He hears your call, He will answer you.*

Isaiah 30:19 NCB

GOODBYE WALLFLOWER WAYS—

If you feel like a fixture, unknown, and *The Problem*, like me, spoiler alert: God is still gracious. This is a good day to cry for help.

DAY 3:
POOR AND NEEDY, LIKE ME? LIKE YOU?

*The poor and needy search for water, but there is none; their
tongues are parched with thirst. But I the L*ORD *will answer them;
I, the God of Israel, will not forsake them. I will make rivers flow
on barren heights, and springs within the valleys. I will turn the
desert into pools of water, and the parched ground into springs.*

Isaiah 41:17-18 NIV

Straight away, my situation turned ugly. The years of not only
feeling like a wallflower but being thrust to the sidelines as a
fixture took a toll. No one noticed me enough to be considered. Even
at church, serving in my own giftings, my only identifiable quality
was to whom I was associated, "This is Cheri Strange. Her husband
is … " Enough was enough. The emotions spilled out. The problem
of me needed to be tackled. But where could I turn? What could Mr.
Perfect do? And who else would believe me or care? Even as someone
who understood a non-specific blanket of love covered her (and "all
the children of the world"), I knew I could turn to God. So turn to
God I did.

Remember the life-changing purchase I made a few pages back?
That turned out to be another notch in my *faltering and failing* belt.
My One Year Bible was getting pulled out as consistently as I knew
how to read it. When you are not convinced you matter and see little
improvement in your situation, it's difficult to believe your efforts
make a difference. (It was not every page, not 365-days with Jesus.
Not even close.) I cried out to the God of those pages in my invisible,
not-what-I-had-in-mind life. My deep emptiness and yearning to
exit this insignificant and obscure place—while not wanting to leave
physically—moved me to take action.

No, I couldn't be in the same league as my super star Mr. Perfect life partner and those like him. I could, however, become a decent, average Christian girl. No one could take that away from me. First on my agenda was to follow the lead of other good Christian girls. I had seen people like this. Every decent, average Christian girl I knew went to a Bible study. No problem. I joined one after work the following week.

It was downtown in a First Baptist Church. There were a whopping five of us in the church library huddled around a twenty-four-inch television screen on a cart. All were twenty years older than I. On the first night, about thirty-five minutes into the lesson, I experienced the beginning of Isaiah 41:17. It was not a conscious awareness, but the words described what was happening to me.

The poor and needy are seeking water, but there is none; Their tongues are parched with thirst, I the LORD, will answer them Myself: I, the God of Israel, will not neglect them. AMP

There was a yearning within I could not articulate, except for the feeling of wanting out. Not to escape the specifics, but to leave the shadows. I ached to be seen, valued and to be more than a fixture. Deep within I hungered for purpose beyond second rate personhood. I wanted to be loved, deeply. Cherished, even. To be indispensable, and intimately known and enjoyed.

What about you? I imagine you know what I mean. Are you longing for personhood? Is it too much to ask to be loved and known by others? Are you thirsty staring at a dry well? This promise is for you today.

I the LORD, will answer them Myself: I, the God of Israel, will not neglect them.

GOODBYE WALLFLOWER WAYS—

Are your longings so deep you have yet to articulate them? Put one to three on paper or technology. Just get it out of your mind and written before you. Pray over it. Maybe you, too, want *out* without leaving physically. Consider these words of Isaiah. Today you may be parched like I was, but you can walk out of the room confident, He will not neglect your need.

DAY 4:
A YEARNING OF EVERY INVISIBLE GIRL

*Come, all you who are thirsty, come to the waters; and you
who have no money, come, buy and eat! Come, buy wine and
milk without money and without cost. Why spend money on
what is not bread, and your labor on what does not satisfy?
Listen, listen to me, and eat what is good, and you will
delight in the richest of fare.*

Isaiah 55:1-2 NIV

No human relationship, perfect partner, well-meaning parent, or
pinky-promise friend can meet the needs generated by the soul
longing to be seen, heard, and known. This same yearning resonates
inside every other invisible girl. These are God-sized desires created
in us so He can fill them first, wholly Himself. In fact, Paul prays for
the Ephesians to "know the love of Christ that surpasses knowledge,"
and he prays they will be "filled with all the fullness of God" (Ephesians 3:19 ESV). But I didn't know then what I now know.

I was a Bible-reading, Jesus-loving believer living out the
American Dream. What more could a person want? Poor in my
affluence. Desperate in my neediness to be seen and known and
loved. You never would have noticed my lack. I didn't dye my hair a
weird color or embrace a flamboyant wardrobe. I was just a regular
girl, like you, staying under the radar, trying not to cause a problem
or be a bother. Thirsty for satisfaction in my life. Seeking happiness
or what might fill my emptiness and coming up dry.

Poor, desperate, and thirsty until I cried out to God in my wrong
theology but in my right yearning. No matter what sort of baggage
you have been preserving, or what bad theology you endorse—no

matter what drama is playing out in your life because of your lack, and regardless of the feelings which might spew out, the God of the Bible is the only One able to meet you in your need. He alone satisfies the thirsty.

Our problem is, we don't like to think of ourselves as needy. I know you. You are the woman who can haul eight shopping bags while pushing the stroller wrapped with the baby in a sling, texting your bestie. Should there be a door between you and the destination, no problem. You've got a hip.

I once watched a mom leaving Target® navigate a toddler, shopping basket and baby to her car, unload her purchases, change the baby's diaper, wrap a present in the back, and put the toddler in the car seat all *with one hand.*

You can organize like a boss or serve a neighbor in need until your fingers ache. Running a business while finishing the laundry, and helping with homework is just a day in the life. You can do so with excellence, without accolades. These skills never cease to amaze.

But ours is a different kind of neediness, with deficits you and I are not equipped to fill. C.S. Lewis reminds us that trying harder or becoming the improved version of ourselves will never work.

> *For mere improvement is not redemption, though redemption always improves people even here and now and will, in the end, improve them to a degree we cannot yet imagine. God became man to turn creatures into sons: not simply to produce better men of the old kind but to produce a new kind of man. It is not like teaching a horse to jump better and better but like turning a horse into a winged creature.*[9]

Yours, Invisible Girl, is a God-sized yearning. You don't possess what it takes in and of yourself. I feel the frustration. I've cried the tears. But I am praying for those days to be long gone. Come along with me and find your path toward becoming seen.

Therefore, if anyone is in Christ, he is a new creation. The old has passed away; behold, the new has come.

2 Corinthians 5:17 ESV

GOODBYE WALLFLOWER WAYS—

If you tote bags of flawed beliefs with buckets of half-healed hurts, decide today to stop looking for satisfaction and healing in all the wrong places. A new improved version of you will never fill your yearnings. Instead, commit to looking to Jesus for what quenches your thirst. He is the only One who can make a new you.

DAY 5:
FAILING FORWARD

The Christian life is very much like climbing a hill of ice.
You cannot slide up, nay, you have to cut every step with an
ice axe; only with incessant labor in cutting and chipping
can you make any progress . . . If you want to know how to
backslide, leave off going forward. Cease going upward and
you will go downward of necessity. You can never stand still.

~Charles H. Spurgeon[10]

Sometimes progress is nothing more than throwing mud at a chain link fence. Most of the mud then falls to the ground, rendering it useless for covering the openings. Wasted. But you keep at it. Eventually enough of the mud sticks to cover all the holes in the fence. You might say it's a work littered with failure upon failure.

Often, progress unfolds by missteps in the same direction. Charles Schulz, the creator of the celebrated *Peanuts* cartoon, submitted some of his drawings to his high school yearbook and even Disney—all were flatly rejected.[11] Steve Jobs was fired from the Apple corporation before later returning to take the company to a nearly two-billion-dollar industry.[12] James Dyson spent years creating 5,126 failed prototypes before designing the first successful dual cyclone bagless vacuum.[13] His was a lot of mud thrown in the same direction, not amounting to anything more than piles of dirt on the ground. (Literally.) Dyson would say all the effort and failed attempts were worth it, as today he is credited with many more inventions and is one of the wealthiest in Britain, worth over eight billion dollars.[14]

These well-known individuals show how failing forward is often the only path toward success, worldly or otherwise. My journey, although spiritual has been vastly the same. Yes. God made me new. But that miraculous act did not leave me Christ-like. To become everything God desires for His own, I had progress to make. There were things to learn and some to unlearn, just like Dyson in finding the right combination of aspects for his inventions. I pictured it as throwing mud on my own chain link fence.

For the next decade, I continued to throw mud at the invisible fence, trying to make spiritual progress and overcome the problem of me. For nine straight years, I repeatedly failed in the same direction by reading the One Year Bible I mentioned before. I pushed ahead toward typifying other Christian girls, unsuccessfully. I skipped nights of Bible study meetings. I left blanks in my workbooks. There were days uncharted. Imperfect? Indubitably. In every way, my path was hit-or-miss for those years. Yet mine, too, was a forward failing. Change was occurring. Somehow, in all my foibles and shortcomings, the mud began to stick. Even amid all those lapses and goof-ups, a regeneration was becoming evident from the inside out.

Allow me to invite you to fail forward, to throw mud at a proverbial chain link fence with tools to help more of the mud stick. To get from Point A to Point B, you don't always need to experience every detour, sundry wanderings, many missteps, and the totality of failures possible. Neither should you recreate the wheel.

I needed more than a decade to hammer out a plan forward to believe God over all else. I'm slow, like a sleepy sloth. Before you lies an offering to keep you centered on the path while providing some structure to cover your fence with mud more quickly and effectively. Throwing mud at a chain link fence and watching only a little stick at a time can be disheartening. It feels like you are not making any progress. But you are. Each time more mud grabs hold of what was thrown before. Slowly and persistently forward movement is made. Before long, whole sections are covered. It's a simple picture of failing forward.

Wouldn't it be great if you had a plan? I cannot give you a different life or bring about the metamorphosis for which you long. This journey will not put you on a path toward fame and favor, but it certainly might help you pinpoint your craving. It can point the thirsty to water, help draw you to the One who sees you in your need, and hold out a cup to help the water to your lips.

Through those repetitive mud-slinging sessions, watching more stick together, covering larger areas, I recognized my own cravings. I realized in Christ, I am no longer limited by what others think, by my own abilities, or anyone's estimation of me. There was a way forward that required my dependence on God as well as my participation. And it was this combination that satisfied my yearnings.

What I thought were nothing more than habit building exercises, tours of duty, and basic spiritual muscle memory rounds, God used to satisfy in me what nothing else ever had. I want to offer you opportunities for slinging some mud onto your own fences.

At first, it might not seem like anything is sticking. It's still the same you hanging close to the sidelines, lonely and passed over. *Keep working at it*. Let it dry. The next time, more mud will cling to the first batch, covering larger and wider parts of the chain in the fence. God can change even you.

You will recognize these adventures as they come under the title, "Failing Forward Feats." Look for your first one right after today's reading. Remember, these are not invitations to attain perfection or to be a better you, but to *fail forward*.

Give it seventy more days. You *can* experience the personal renovation for which you long.

Call to me and I will answer you, and will tell you great and hidden things that you have not known.

Jeremiah 33:3 ESV

GOODBYE WALLFLOWER WAYS—

Have you ever experienced progress despite a failure? How do the lives and experiences of these who have accomplished such greatness amid astounding failures influence your willingness to move forward, even if it means failing? I know it can be scary, but moving away from the walls of your life is going to require courage to fail. Today, I'm praying for you.

> *Lord, give my friend the willingness, courage, and strength to take the next step to become visible, even if it's scary. Give her the grace to get up when she falls, knowing all efforts toward progress are forward failings. And these, You can use for Your glory. Amen.*

DAY 6:
FAILING FORWARD FEAT #1

The Word of God well understood and religiously
obeyed is the shortest route to spiritual perfection.
And we must not select a few favorite passages to the
exclusion of others. Nothing less than a whole Bible
can make a whole Christian.

~A.W. Tozer[15]

There has been no greater transformational move in my life, outside of accepting Jesus as my Savior, than getting into the habit of reading the Bible every day, every year. It's not hip, revolutionary, or exciting. Neither is breathing nor eating or brushing our teeth. But we do these daily because they are life-sustaining. (Maybe not brushing your teeth, unless you have someone in your life with gum disease, like us. Then even brushing your teeth becomes critical, but still not exciting.)

Today, get yourself a One Year Bible. Or download a free version online at https://oneyearbibleonline.com/reading-plan-downloads/ and print a schedule. Sign up for a 365-day Bible reading plan on Bible.com or the YouVersion app. You can even listen to it while you get ready. Or pull out Old Faithful—that Bible you've had for years—and make your own plan for the next year. There are many options available to help you sling this mud.

Let's say you are concerned you can't get past the download. Start smaller. Plan to read a book of the Bible from start to finish. Make your plan to read for fifteen minutes every day. Be prepared to fail. And keep going forward. It's a small decision that could change your life forever.

Often, I purchase used books. I don't mind because only the first two or three pages tend to contain markings or comments. Beyond that, it's clean and crisp. Clearly, the previous owner had good intentions when they started. But they didn't get far before they quit. Maybe you will fail, too. Likely, you will, just like I did.

Don't quit.

I repeat.

Do not stop slinging mud. Remember, it's a chain link fence. It's going to take a lot of mud and a whole lot of effort over time to close the gaps, giving that mud time to cover the holes. Even when you fail, keep in mind, it's a failing *forward*.

One does not surrender a life in an instant. That which is lifelong can only be surrendered in a lifetime."

~Elisabeth Elliot[16]

Remember, in the back of this book, you will find a section called, "My Personal Plan for Becoming Invincible," because you becoming spiritually invincible is the aim. Starting with this activity, the plan walks through the rest of the book, helping you design your own plan for moving forward. It's simple to follow along if you would like to work through it while you read the book. There is not a task for each day, but each is numbered so that it is easily identified. Or if you would prefer to do it when you finish reading, feel free. It's really up to you.

Either way, do not forget to tell us how it's going on social media by using the hashtag #failingforward. A whole group of fellow forward movers will be waiting for you, cheering you on.

CHAPTER 2

THE "UNS" HAVE IT

When you are down to nothing, God is up to something.

~Babbie Mason[17]

Chances are, you understand all too well my overall sense of invisibility. Your story will be different from mine, but those wallflower tendencies lead us to the same desolate place.

Looking back, I realize I could have remained there—hidden, feeling inferior, less than, and ineffective. But God was up to something. Through the raw emotions I have experienced along with the circumstances that led to my sense of being invisible, God met me. Across the next few days, I continue to invite you to meet me in my story. Oh, how I pray God meets you in yours.

Day 7:
Throwback to Middle School Gym Class

I've never run into a person who yearns for their
middle school days.

~Jeff Kinney[18]

Remember Hagar? She is the Egyptian slave of Sarah, the wife of Abraham. Abraham received the promise from God announcing his descendants would outnumber the stars, they would possess the land of Canaan, and an heir would be born from his own body (Genesis 15:4-7). There seems to be a problem with the promise. Sarah and Abraham are old enough to get senior discounts everywhere, committed for life, and childless for decades.

Maybe Sarah figured since God did not name her in the promise (Genesis 13:16), and because she has gone through menopause (making it physically impossible for her to conceive an heir) (Genesis 12:4), the promise must mean Abraham and *someone else*. This servant named Hagar becomes Sarah's best idea for seeing the prophecy fulfilled. The wife gives the younger Egyptian woman to the husband as a secondary wife to have a baby as a culturally acceptable last resort effort (Genesis 16).

What could go wrong?

Any girl who has survived her middle school locker room years and lived to tell tales could smell the trouble brewing like last year's forgotten gym bag. As expected, it was only a matter of months before a brouhaha ensued. When Hagar learned she was pregnant, she flaunted her newfound hifalutin position in Sarah's face. As you might expect, the actual wife didn't take this heckling on the sidelines, and some classic girl drama unfolded.

The tables turned on the haughty heir-carrying Egyptian who hoped to dethrone the rightful wife. Her malfeasant behavior took her out of secondary wife status and plunged her back into servitude with Abraham's blessing. It was more than she could endure. Ultimately, Hagar escaped the messy theatrics. She arrived in the desert, discarded, thirsty, and alone.

She shouldn't matter. The Egyptian woman was a bona fide nobody. But God had other plans for this thrown-away slave girl. In fact, she had an experience most of us would envy. The angel of the LORD found her by a spring of water in the wilderness (Genesis 16:7).

And he said, "Hagar, servant of Sarai, where have you come from and where are you going?"

Genesis 16:8 ESV.

He can locate you in your desert mess as well. Nobody or otherwise, the Lord will find you as he did Hagar. He seeks you in your aloneness, in the wreckage of your own making, or while you're fleeing to the desert, metaphorically or actually. He's coming for you.

For the Son of Man came to seek and to save the lost.

Luke 19:10 ESV

GOODBYE WALLFLOWER WAYS–

It's a valid inquiry from the angel to Hagar. *Where have you come from and where are you going?* Thinking in spiritual terms, how would you respond? Do you know God will come for you?

DAY 8:
(Un)Seen by the God Who Sees

You are the God who sees me.

Genesis 16:13 NIV

Conceivably, this girl Hagar has not even voiced a single prayer. There is no prior evidence she even believed in the God of Abraham. Not to mention her entire predicament was on Him. Her misery would not be a cause to call upon the God under whom she suffers. She's simply on the run, trying to escape the bitter episode. This woman wanted to be free. But the desert was her only consolation.

Still, in this desperate place of desertion and utter abandonment, God found her. Hagar. He did not go seeking humanity at large. God was not on a mission to save a random group of people in the desert, and she happened among them. The girl is an Egyptian, for heaven's sake. She's not even one of God's chosen people. She's not even supposed to get an invitation to the prom. Yet, God[19] called this throwaway slave girl, one who was a mere sidebar in the narrative, not even a key player, *by name.*

Not only did He call her by name, but He gave her specific instructions to follow: to return and submit to Sarah. For the first time, so it may have seemed, happenstance did not rule her life. She had a purpose and a promise worth aiming toward. She was going to bear a son whose name would be Ishmael, because the Lord paid attention to her suffering (Genesis 16:11).

No, Hagar had not prayed. We cannot even be sure she believed in God. She was an Egyptian. But it didn't matter. Her Creator did not overlook her suffering, even at the hands of His own people. Regardless of Hagar's words, beliefs, or actions, God pursued the runaway no one else would chase after. He called her by name and offered her purpose, along with an exceedingly great promise.

After their conversation regarding the child she was carrying and her need to return and submit to Sarah, Hagar said, "You are the God who sees me" (Genesis 16:13 ESV). She was not acknowledging God's omniscience, as if to say, "I recognize I am one of thousands upon thousands you allow to grace your presence. I'm thankful to be a part of all God's children. These are general revelations, I'm sure, applicable to everyone." No. That was my bad theology, not the misconceptions of the insignificant godless slave girl.

Hagar's was a personal encounter by a God who is omniscient. Knowing all, yet familiar with her—fully. He had been watching, so He knew her situation. Her suffering came as no surprise. Her sin was not a shocker. The shirked responsibilities and broken relationships were unhidden. Her whereabouts were identifiable to Him before she arrived. Insignificant Hagar was seen. She was no longer invisible. And it changed the course of her life.

He sees you as well. You are not insignificant to Him. You are seen.

As for you, LORD, you know me; you see me.

Jeremiah 12:3 CSB

GOODBYE WALLFLOWER WAYS—

Write these words for yourself. Place them where you can get them into the marrow of your bones: *You are the God who sees me.* Because He is. And He does.

Day 9:
Seen as Ordinary

All I have seen teaches me to trust the Creator for all
I have not seen.

~Ralph Waldo Emerson[20]

Perhaps you have picked up this book, overwhelmed by a per-ceived sense of worthlessness. Maybe there is the slight belief you, like Hagar, could hightail it to the desert with no one in pursuit.

Don't do it.

Recognize the same omniscient God pursues even you. He knows your whereabouts better than your phone. God pursues you in your hurt, in your misery, your suffering, and your rejection. Whether someone has done the offense to you or your wounds are self-inflicted, or even imagined, the reality remains the same. God sees you. Not you, as a people group or in your ethnicity. You are not a cause to uphold, a project, or someone He has to love because He is God. Your Father has been acquainted with the intricacies of you, as an individual in your lame jokes, chipped tooth, and love of big dogs, since before you were born (Psalm 139:13). You, the baseball game going, gum-smacking, quilt-making, picture-taking, sleep-deprived, latte drinking, Christmas movie junkie. Whatever defines you, God sees everything encompassing your person to the minutia, including the number of hairs on your head today (Luke 12:7). Not a day in your life has remained hidden (Psalm 139:14-16). In fact, Him *not* seeing you is an impossible feat.

Never mind your lousy behavior. Maybe, like Hagar, you haven't even prayed. It doesn't matter. God cannot *not* see you. He comes after you. He pursues you in your backslidden, mistake-ridden, pain-infused, humiliated, and stuck-in-impossible-circumstances self. It might be a repelling sight, but He takes notice of you. There is something beautiful, and comforting, and peace-ushering when we recognize this truth about God and our relationship with Him.

Hagar was a minor player—hers may have been considered a throwaway life of servitude. Yet the omniscient, all-seeing God pursues this life of insignificance way out into the desert. He appears to her personally and gives purpose to her life with an incredible promise. If God will do this for someone like Hagar, He has purpose, mission, and promise for your life, as well. Not only, my friend, are you not outside of His vision, but He's also inviting you to dance.

Can a man hide himself in secret places so that I cannot see him? declares the LORD. *Do I not fill heaven and earth? declares the* LORD.

Jeremiah 23:24 ESV

GOODBYE WALLFLOWER WAYS–

Grab your phone. Turn up some tunes and dance. Dance like the God of the universe is watching. And His eyes are all that matters.

Day 10:
(Un)Heard by the God Who Hears

Can you see me? Can you hear me? Does anything I say
mean anything to you?

~Oprah Winfrey[21]

Hagar is not the only one who finds herself amid domestic may-
hem. Another woman in the Bible lands at sixes and sevens,
as well. Hannah encounters some drama of her own. She married a
man named Elkanah, who also married someone else concurrently (1
Samuel 1:1-2). A perfect composition for marital bliss it is not. This
someone else, named Peninnah, assumed a position of superiority
over Hannah because she has children, as if she has something to do
with it (1 Samuel 1:6). Hannah does not have children. And here we
are, back in the middle school locker room. The drama intensifies so
greatly, the Bible describes the other wife as Hannah's enemy who
"used to provoke her grievously to irritate her . . . year by year. As
often as they went to the house of the LORD ...." (1 Samuel 1:6-7
ESV).

Our girl, Hannah, acts contrary to Hagar and even Sarah. She
does not rush to gain support from her girlfriends. Our hurting
friend refrains from seeking reinforcement from anyone who will
line up on her side to malign her enemy. She doesn't complain to her
husband about the tormenting competitor, nor does she hightail it to
the desert to escape her lot in life. After years of malicious tackiness
from her rival and unfulfilled longings for God to give her a child,
Hannah does the only thing she knows to do. She prays her guts out
before the Lord (I Samuel 1:11).

Hannah prays so intently the priest notes her behavior (1
Samuel 1:13). Upon exiting one of Peninnah's sessions of vexation,

this poor woman is further wronged by being accused by the highest authority in her life of being drunk in the temple. After she explains her desperate conduct as a distraught heart calling upon the Lord, asking God to hear her, the priest, Eli, responds. He prays for God to grant her request. He prays for God to hear her (1 Samuel 1:17). And God does.

When Hannah returns to the tabernacle again, a child accompanies her. To this same priest she says, "I prayed for this child, and the LORD has granted me what I asked of him" (I Samuel 1:27 NIV).

In other words, "Remember me? I'm the one you thought was drunk as a skunk in church. But I was so desperately praying. And you prayed God would grant my request. Well, here he is. God heard my petition. Here stands the evidence that God listened to me, personally."

And this is the confidence that we have toward him, that if we ask anything according to his will he hears us.

1 John 5:14 ESV

GOODBYE WALLFLOWER WAYS—

Maybe God has allowed you to come to this place, like Hannah, so that you will pray out of an earnestness for Him to hear you. Be sure to do so before your head hits the pillow tonight. And maybe, through this insignificant second wife, God has assured you He does, indeed, hear you.

Day 11:
Fairytale Yearnings

The minute that you bring a unicorn into a story, you know
that it's a fairy tale or a fable, because unicorns don't exist as
animals. They exist as fantasy creatures.

~Gloria Vanderbilt[22]

Honestly, my glass-is-half-empty mentality is quick to dismiss
Hannah and her experiences recorded in black and white. Her
story can read more like a fairytale to a person like me, with a bow
tying up all the loose ends, complete with the happy ending. In my
mind, all it's missing is a unicorn. What about the times when it
doesn't work out so orderly? How about those instances when we
have prayed our guts out and God has not granted our request? Suppose God hears the Hannahs who have important roles to fulfill but
not the ordinary wallflowers like you and me? These are the questions
rolling through the head of a person stuck in the shadows of her
own life, uncertain God hears her. Wallflowers scarred by rejection,
insecurities, and snubbings are prone to dismiss Pollyanna narratives
like these.

The problem with my negativity is how impossible it is to stand
up against the evidence. Scripture shows us God's attentiveness to
prayer doesn't stop at Hannah and her storybook outcome. The
affirmation God hears and responds to the prayers of His people turns
up repeatedly. From Abraham (Genesis 18:22-33) to Moses (Exodus
33:11), David (2 Samuel 7:4-16) to Habakkuk (Habakkuk 2:2-3)
to prisoners in jail cells (Acts 23:11), and from misfit nobodies—
wallflowers whose names aren't mentioned—God hears the pleas of

His people. He gives His ear to women in the shadows like you and me, answering them specifically when called.

The invitation for individuals like me who see the cup as half empty, my fellow fairytale-yearning shrinking violets, is to follow Hannah's example after all. For Jesus Himself bids us to "Ask, and it will be given to you; seek, and you will find; knock, and it will be opened to you. For everyone who asks receives, and the one who seeks finds, and to the one who knocks it will be opened" (Matthew 7:7-8 ESV). Beyond Hannah's narrative are promises and assurances galore bidding you and me to be heard. You cannot stand far off enough to go unnoticed. There is no one outside of the invitation to come boldly to the throne of grace. Here you will find an open hand of mercy and grace to help you in your time of need.

Let us then with confidence draw near to the throne of grace, that we may receive mercy and find grace to help in time of need.

Hebrews 4:16 ESV

He not only sees you, my friend, He's leaning in to hear what is on your heart.

GOODBYE WALLFLOWER WAYS—

"What sort of God wants to lean in and listen to a person like me?" you might ask. That's the unicorn-seeking wallflower talking. Dismiss her. She's no longer welcome here. Your God is listening and longing to hear what you say. Go on and keep telling him. Go bold!

DAY 12:
BAD THEOLOGY UNPACKED

No Christian can avoid theology. Everyone has a theology.
The issue, then, is not, do we want to have a theology?
That's a given. The real issue is, do we have a sound
theology? Do we embrace true or false doctrine?

~R.C. Sproul[23]

My theology had sprung largely out of the music I learned in my childhood. It developed from songs like "He's Got the Whole World in His Hands."

> He's got everybody here in His hands,
>
> He's got everybody there in His hands,
>
> He's got everybody everywhere in His hands,
>
> He's got the whole world in His hands.[24]

And what a wonderful message to have deeply ingrained. It sounds so appealing, doesn't it? Everybody. Everywhere. As the song goes, so continued my mistaken understanding. I doubt I'm alone in latching onto unfounded beliefs from a sweet, inclusive melody like this one.

It's so hard to believe, isn't it? I mean, if you are accustomed to being excluded from the A Team or stuck in your emotional corner, it doesn't seem like God could attend to such marginal side-sitters.

Somehow, this melody from the children's song navigated into the core of my theology, communicating the same thing we find in the middle school locker room, or the lunchroom, the youth group at most churches I attended, and my college friend experience.

My struggle did not lie with the foundational inclusivity of the song. Unequivocally, God loves His own with unconditional love. The very essence of God is love (1 John 4:7). But the song didn't tell the complete story. At least, I didn't believe so. There remained a group of people who seemed to have a direct line to more. More I was not invited to experience. More in terms of relationship, intimacy in prayer, in depth of knowledge, and what I considered super-secret privileged Christian stuff. For all that, you had to be an insider. Qualified. Chosen. Oozing with talents and brains. Oh, I was welcome to hang on the outskirts, but I didn't pass the smell test for being an insider.

These lyrical misgivings had become ingrained from years of obedient church going mixed with spotty devotion to Christ. My life experiences lined up with my theology. Therefore, I believed it all the more.

The problem with an interpretation like mine and its application to the Christian life is its categorical inaccuracy. Absolute hogwash. In fact, I have never been more wrong about anything in my life. My super-secret Christian mumbo jumbo understandings were a string of untruths I allowed myself to believe because they fit with my experiences. It was when I started encountering Truth on my own and spending time in Bible study made for the ordinary everyday Christian, the unpacking of my bad theology began.

When I studied Ephesians, I began to see the promises and privileges God offers to ordinary, insecure nobodies like myself, the first of which was His love. There was no distinction in the language. No special, secret prayer reserved for the elite Christian club. Paul earnestly desired every believer in Christ to possess a love so rich, so deep, that it exceeds understanding.

For this reason I bow my knees before the Father . . . that
you, being rooted and grounded in love, may have strength

to comprehend with all the saints what is the breadth and
length and height and depth, and to know the love of Christ
that surpasses knowledge, that you may be filled with all the
fullness of God.

Ephesians 3:14, 17-19 ESV

Somehow the power of those words made their way into my collection of faulty understandings and ingrained beliefs so that I received them as Truth. There it was. Gospel hope, right on the page. For me. No, it was not my experience. I felt zero warm fuzzies. Just a faint hope ushering in enough momentum for me to begin unpacking my bad theology and replacing it with what the Bible actually said.

Maybe you've rallied around some faulty understandings of your own. Maybe, like me, you read God's promises into others. But He couldn't mean you. There are too many mistakes. Lost battles. Wrong turns. Wasted years. Squandered resources. I mean, what's He really got to work with anyway, right? Compared to… her?

It's time to do some unpacking. Let me help you.

I pray today, Lord, on this page, that my friend
will look at Your Words as meant for her. Preserved.
Intentional. Personal. Give her Gospel hope
enough to provide what she needs to unpack any
misunderstandings or untruths about You.

GOODBYE WALLFLOWER WAYS—

Write three beliefs you hold about God or how you believe He views you. Not what you *should* believe, but what plays out by your experience. Be honest. Put these in a place you can locate later.

DAY 13:
THE HARD WAY

And he had to pass through Samaria.

John 4:4 ESV

John (in chapter 4, verses 1-42) tells us about another woman like me who had a few things wrong. This woman doesn't even get a name. We simply know her as "the Samaritan woman" or "the woman at the well." She gets those distinctions because they were obvious and because society in those days deemed her worth about the same as a couple of goats or a cow. She is a Samaritan by heritage (which Jews deemed as half-breeds or dogs, for intermarrying with the Assyrians in disobedience to the law in Deuteronomy 7:3-5)[25], and Jesus meets her by a well as she comes to draw water. John tells us Jesus *had* to go through Samaria on this occasion. (Although, geographically, He did not. Jews typically took the long way around as not to have any involvement with Samaritans.) This necessary meeting is not because this woman is a member of the super-secret elite Christian club I had made up. She's not even an average Christian side-sitter. Religious? Yes. But as the story unfolds, this woman is a nobody, more like you and me, with her own imaginary bundle of badness strapped to her back, filled with disappointments, heartbreak, and bad theology.

Here was a girl who had legitimate sour grapes regarding fairytales, unicorns, and the illusions of happy endings, including the promised Messiah. She had every reason to find her place along the outskirts. Understand, this woman knew a thing or two about rejection, exclusion, abandonment, and not being valued by those closest to her. Before the day is out, we learn she has married five times and is living with guy number six (John 4:18).

Why does a woman, worth little more than livestock in her culture, end up rejected by five happily ever after hopefuls? Notice, this is not the twenty-first century. No-fault divorce courts are not on every corner. She has zero rights. The man holds all the cards. If he wants her out, she's out. Five times a covenant promise is broken. Five times she is rejected and abandoned. Five times her hopes are smashed by failure upon failure, rejection after rejection, humiliation upon humiliation.

Was she a temptress? Ravishing? Flirtatious? Did she bring her trouble upon herself? Was she simply selfish or boring or a terrible cook? We don't know. What we can surmise is the understanding that most women marry with the fairytale ending in mind. "Until death do us part" remains the hope-filled aspect of the covenant. And when this commitment is broken, no matter the circumstance, pain ensues. The remnants of past rejection and abandonment fuel the fear of future dismissals building barriers between the one cast off and the rest of the world. She becomes more insulated from further injury. By husband number five, the emotional walls are likely high. After him, ain't nobody getting in. She's not worth keeping. She might as well be the tramp. Living with man number six fits with her narrative.

Sometimes we come by our wallflower ways the hard way. Through pain and hurts resembling those of our unnamed Samaritan friend, we assemble our baggage and strap it on our backs. You and I try to make sense of what we believe based on what we know and what we have been through. Most of the time, that line of reasoning leads us down a path lacking in hope, absent of faith, holding to a general distrust.

Thankfully, this woman still got thirsty. And there was only one well.

On the last day of the feast, the great day, Jesus stood up and cried out, "If anyone thirsts, let him come to me and drink.

John 7:37 ESV

GOODBYE WALLFLOWER WAYS—

Think about your own personal failures that have landed in your bucket of badness. Jot them down. Remember, badness and misunderstandings did not keep Jesus from this "good-for-nothing" woman. He will meet you where you are as well. Confess the badness. Throw the paper away. Wallflower, you are not what you have done.

Day 14:
(Un)Known by the God Who Knows

The God who created, names and numbers the stars in
the heavens also numbers the hairs of my head. He pays
attention to very big things and to very small ones. What
matters to me matters to Him, and that changes my life.

~Elizabeth Elliot[26]

It is here, at the well, our Samaritan friend's bad theology unravels. From John's Gospel account (4:1-42), we read of Jesus having to go through Samaria. He *had* to go through Samaria, not because it was the traditional path for traveling Jews (it wasn't), but because a rejected half-breed female was thirsty, looking for water, in the same place she had always found it. This trip to the well, however, would be different. Like Hagar, Jesus meets this woman at a well in her need. And like Hagar, the throwaway slave girl, He came in pursuit of this woman. She wasn't even seeking or praying or hoping. It was simply her in her mess, looking for water.

The encounter seems sort of awkward. He asks her for a drink. His is a shocking request. Jesus explains how she should, in fact, be asking *Him* for a drink so she can have living water (John 4:10). The practical woman she is, she notices the man has nothing with which to draw water. She throws this factoid back at Him in an almost snarky manner, asking Him where, precisely, does He get this so-called *living water?* Who exactly does He think He is (John 4:11-12)? Jesus, unmoved, continues to explain the living water analogy, conveying the life-giving truth the water He is promising to give will become in the person "a spring of water welling up to eternal life"

(John 4:14 ESV). Intrigued, the woman comes on board to ask Him for this water, as He suggested in the beginning. And this is when Jesus touches a pressure point.

Jesus said to her, "Go, call your husband, and come here."

John 4:16 ESV

She honestly admits to not having a husband. Jesus, of course, knows this. Next, He tells her what she had not shared. There have been five husbands. She is currently unwed and living with number six. There she stood, exposed. To get away from the humiliation of the moment, she changes the subject to theology. She has some theological misgivings of her own. But in the end, Jesus clears the fog by declaring to her, personally, who He is.

The woman said to him, "I know that Messiah is coming (he who is called Christ). When he comes, he will tell us all things." Jesus said to her, "I who speak to you am he."

John 4:25-26 ESV

What is His point in exposing this woman's shame? Humiliation? Dominance? No. Nothing like it. No longer thirsty, she leaves her jar and heads back home to her neighborhood. Hear what she announces about her encounter with Jesus.

"Come, see a man who told me all that I ever did. Can this be the Christ?"

John 4:29 ESV

What she needed was to be known. Truly known, bare faced and unhidden, without fear of being overlooked, betrayed, indicted, or discarded because she didn't matter. She did matter. Jesus *had* to go through Samaria. He had to because Jesus knew an unnamed, degenerate woman was about to be thirsty and needed to be shown she was known. All of her. Not the beautiful outside part. Not the allure that attracted six men to devote themselves to her, at least for a while. Everything. The rejected, worthless, used, and lonely person underneath the outer shell. The girl who came to the well alone. Shunned by others. Rejected by many. Thirsty. The long-awaited Savior came after *her*. And He knew her personally, with all the dirt.

Will number six discard her? Maybe. Maybe not. Will he be willing to marry her after all? Who knows? But no longer is her value wrapped up in someone else's estimation of her. The Savior of the world revealed Himself to *her*. He knew all the ugly. It was ghastly. Yet it didn't move Him. Jesus loved her still. We don't even know the name of this bad girl. She is otherwise insignificant. Jesus did. He went looking for this certain woman and her alone.

I hope you are catching on. Same story, third verse. There is a freedom and comfort and vivacity in this deep level of being known by the Savior, which is nothing short of inexplicable. And it is written, explained, and declared for you to embrace. You, my friend, are known by the God who knows.

> *O Lord, you have searched me and known me!*
>
> Psalm 139:1 ESV

GOODBYE WALLFLOWER WAYS—

What is it you need to know that God knows? Is it that you exist? That He cares about you, specifically? He knows what you have been through and is still sovereign over it? That you matter as a person? Still? Read Psalm 139:1-6 and write what these verses communicate to you about God knowing you.

Day 15:
Dangerous Failing Forward Adventuring

Be sober-minded; be watchful. Your adversary the devil
prowls around like a roaring lion, seeking someone to devour.

1 Peter 5:8 ESV

The mud was sticking on my fence. Like this woman from Samaria, my circumstances did not change. Oh, I was still invisible. As I had been, I continued to be the Super Star's wife. Yet over time, I had come to recognize Jesus knew me in the same inexplicable ways. In my thirsty moments, He came looking for me. No, it didn't happen for me in the desert, nor did I have a Jacob's Well experience. I didn't fall out in the Spirit or have a special revelation in my dreams. Maybe He will meet you in those ways, but for me, it was much more ordinary. It was unimpressive, mediocre me, continuing to leave my inconsistent ways behind.

Through my failing forward adventures, I came to understand the same truths only *Living Water* can bring. Certain people were not loved more (Ephesians 3:17-19), even if I was treated that way at times. God did not have less for me than anyone else (Ephesians 2:8-10), even if this was other people's perception of my talents and abilities, or even my personality. What matters is understanding there are great and precious promises given to every believer in Christ to be individually enjoyed and exercised (Ephesians 1:17-19). I had left these untapped.

I found consolation through the obscure, the supporting cast, the people no one would miss if they didn't show up, and those rejected by even their inner circle. Because God saw, He heard, and He knew them. The God of the universe did not stand with hands spread wide, holding the masses of humanity, nameless, faceless, loving them without distinction, as I surmised. The "un's" had won me over: the unknowns, the unnamed, the unsuccessful, the unimportant, and the unseen. Those who felt marginalized and invisible—just like me, were intimately known by the One who loves us best. Yes. The mud was, indeed, beginning to cover my fence.

For each of us who struggle with a wallflower mentality, this is an internal battle with the enemy (1 Peter 5:8). If Satan can keep you messed up from your childhood or your beliefs, swimming around in bad theology—thinking God is holding out on you or glossing over you, certain He doesn't have plans for your life, convinced you are forgotten, useless, better left as a wallflower—then you won't be a problem.

But let your thirst for more lead you to *Living Water*, throw mud on your own chain link fence, and catch wind of the truth God has for your life? Girl, you will single-handedly become dangerous. At any age. Any stage of life. Any ethnicity or socioeconomic distinction. Your God never intended for you to be invisible, my friend. Know today He sees you. He hears your heart. He is familiar with all the intricacies about you. And He loves you more than you can imagine.

Sanctify them in the truth; your word is truth.

John 17:17 ESV

GOODBYE WALLFLOWER WAYS—

Today is simple: Pray that God will help you distinguish truth about Him from lies. Voice this prayer regularly.

Day 16:
Invisible No More

I believe that God has a plan and purpose not only for the
human race, but for my individual life.

~Anne Graham Lotz[27]

Dude Perfect is a favorite show at our house. Not only are the
guys on the show believers, two of the team members are twins,
much like my boys, and the group originated from Texas A&M, my
husband's alma mater. We love the show because the guys attempt
wild and wily feats in clever, clean, and creative ways. Recently, one
adventure included spending the night in a sporting goods store. In
the morning, the owner gave the keys of the store to these guys with
the instructions that they could take home anything they could carry
within a set time limit. They made off with more items imaginable
pulled in kayaks, rafts, and anything else that could pull their haul.

When I sensed the truths we've been expressing—about God
and myself—becoming realities in my life, forget sporting goods.
It was as if someone handed me the master keys to an outlet mall
with permission to take anything I could carry home in a semitrailer
without the time limits! It seemed almost too good to be true. But
one thing was certain. I took hold of the invisible keys. Keeping the
old status quo was no longer an option. Those beliefs and actions
and attitudes once latched onto my person, weighing me down, and
holding me in a death grip no longer held such power. I loaded my
hands and heart with something better. I was invisible no more.

It was on this journey I found my voice. Not the sort that tries
to topple every other to be heard, but the one God created to show
His superbness through my gifting. This struggle unearthed my
worth. God's Truth revealed in me changed me from the inside out.

58

My need for your approval lost its grip on me, and social media's promises lost their enchantment. It's where I recognized my sin in manifold ways, especially the sin of unbelief. Here I also discovered forgiveness and restoration and soul-soothing, satisfying a thirst I had longed for all my days.

My vision of what my life could be had been narrow and limited. But it was in this mud-slinging process God taught me the discipline and joys of intimacy. Significance and purpose were mine beyond measure. I no longer needed to stand in the shadows or find my place on the sidelines. No longer did I keep quiet, or assume God could use others but not me. All this from a person you've never heard of, whose only mark in life results from her associations. The *more* I longed for was available for wallflowers like me. I am living proof there is Gospel hope for the woman nobody notices.

Because of this tremendous work God has shown He can do in the likes of throwaway nobodies, insignificant players whose names we don't even know, and the wives of super stud husbands no one cares to even mention, you, too, can say goodbye to your wallflower ways. You can become invisible no more.

I do not cease to give thanks for you, remembering you in my prayers, that the God of our Lord Jesus Christ, the Father of glory, may give you the Spirit of wisdom and of revelation in the knowledge of him, having the eyes of your hearts enlightened, that you may know what is the hope to which he has called you ...

Ephesians 1:16-18 ESV

GOODBYE WALLFLOWER WAYS—

These verses from Paul exude with good news. Write out Ephesians 1:16-18, writing your name in place of every "you." It might sound awkward, but these verses are for you. They are personal promises given to every believing wallflower to help her say, "So long. I've stayed here too long. I'm putting my wallflower ways behind me."

Day 17:
Failing Forward Feat #2

The Lord is near to all who call on him to all who call on him in truth.

Psalm 145:18 ESV

*D*raw near.

We are going to look more at prayer in days to come, but I would be remiss if I didn't make it a priority in our failing forward adventures. Like other aspects of the Christian life, prayer develops over time. Honestly, it's not as difficult as it feels. You possess the privilege to take anything and everything before God anywhere at any time. It's that open. But if you are like me, having such freedom actually results in failure. If prayer is so open and available, I don't have it in my routine so I end up not praying. The other urgent things overtake all that freedom in my life.

To draw near to God, you and I need a strategy for praying. Let's make it simple and practical. Pick a time and a place. Plan to spend fifteen minutes praying. Be there every day.

Pick a time: Don't be crazy. If you have never been one to get up at 5:00 a.m. do not set your new prayer time at that time to pray for an hour. Be realistic. If you want to pray in the morning and there is no margin for it, set an achievable goal. Get up fifteen minutes earlier. Think about the time you spend on social media, reading news, shopping for what you don't need, or doing other non-essentials on your phone or computer. Maybe you can look at your schedule and find the time within your day that can be exchanged for praying.

Once you decide on a time, **pick a place**. Try to pick one that provides solitude, without interruption. It doesn't need to be pretty or even clean. Plan to be there every day. If you forget, go the first time you can get free. The goal is to sling mud. Establish the habit. This is what you do because your God is listening. He is waiting to hear what you have to say. In fact, He can't wait for you to decide when and where to get started.

When you decide when and where, after praying one day, drop your when and where (like 9:15am, playroom) on social media using the hashtag #falingforward. We will know what you mean and celebrate your win.

CHAPTER 3

IS CHANGE POSSIBLE?

Are you wondering if change is possible? Could it really become your reality to live seen, heard, loved, and known? About right now it might feel as doable as finishing a marathon because you stared at the training schedule, or building an airplane with scrap metal and duct tape.

Left unto ourselves, a cynical sense is on target. Yes. Change is possible. But no, you can't usher it into your own life at will. And that's a good thing.

> "You would not have called to me unless I had been calling to you," said the Lion.
>
> ~C.S. Lewis[28]

How is it we become visible? We are not talking about popularity, becoming the center of attention or dominating Instagram. Although, there is a type of visibility for which we are aiming—the kind where your name, your position, and the accolades which might accompany it may blend into the scenery, but who you are and the One you represent become unmistakably conspicuous.

This type of visibility is wrought with a paradox of its own. The prophet Isaiah writes:

This is what the LORD says,

"In a favorable time I have answered You, And in a day of salvation I have helped You. And I will keep watch over You and give You for a covenant of the people,

To restore the land [from its present state of ruin] and to apportion and give as inheritances the deserted hereditary lands,

Saying to those who are bound and captured, 'Go forth, And to those who are in [spiritual] darkness, 'Show yourselves,' [come into the light of the Savior] ... "

Isaiah 49:8-9 AMP

Such prominence cannot surface by holding up the wall in the shadows. Change is possible. The invitation is for you and me to, instead, *Go and Show.* Venture out into your houses, your jobs, and your neighborhoods showing how God is impassioning your life. The rest of the book is your guide to finding the strategies necessary for becoming invincible. I aim to help you craft a workable plan, personal while effective for bringing you out of the shadows. Without changing your circumstances, the tools contained here will help equip you to better embrace your purpose. This is both spiritual and practical. Even if other people treat you the same old way, God willing, as you implement your plan, you will not remain the same. No longer will you be unseen, for this is the Gospel in you. The time is here to become visible, to *Go and Show.*

DAY 18:
BECOMING THE ZEBRA

In the same way, let your light shine before others, so that they may see your good works and give glory to your Father who is in heaven.

Matthew 5:16 ESV

"Would someone please stop turning off the lights?"

I bellow these words every few days. It seems I'm raising green teens or rule followers. I have taught my eight children to conserve energy, yes. But every day, there is a constant flicker as people enter and exit rooms, creating a disco in my living room, then the stairs, even the laundry room. Every time I need to see, the lights are off, making it nigh on impossible.

When a person feels shut down, unimportant, and like the lights have been turned off on them, that's often when they move into wallflower mode. But this is not how Jesus wants us to live. To His disciples He points out that a person would never light a lamp only to cover it up (Matthew 5:15). What pure silliness. Instead, you would put the light out in the open, upon its stand where it belongs, ensuring others could see it and see by it.

It's at least as absurd to think our place is blending into the surroundings as it is to light a lamp only to conceal it. We will unequivocally miss the intended purpose Jesus has for our lives if we remain hidden, by choice or by hindrance, like turning off a switch or putting a lamp under a bowl.

What does it look like in the hurly-burly of real life to see yourself as a lamp that gives light to the room? Stark contrast, for certain. You and I should be like the lamp post lighting up the parking lot when the mall has closed. Instantly, every inch of light we offer someone is essential for getting them home safely.

It's the glaring contrast between a lone zebra standing in the middle of a pasture surrounded by ordinary brown cows. Unless you are on safari in Africa, or on a wildlife preserve, a zebra is going to stand out in any field this side of the Atlantic.

Picture this hayfield with me. The scene is peaceful, somewhat ordinary: cows grazing, chewing their cud, swinging their tails at the flies, enjoying herd life. Suddenly something else seizes your attention. At first, you think you are hallucinating. It cannot be. You blink, turn away, shake yourself. Yet, the object remains. Amid the everyday rural tranquility stands something entirely different. A solitary zebra positions itself among the brown cows, doing pretty much what the others are doing. Eating grass. Swatting at the flies landing on its back. Enjoying life in the pasture. Except it's not what we were expecting to see. The sight is captivating.

It may surprise you to know my illustration is not as far-fetched as one might think. Texas is the home of an unregulated number of zebras in recent days. These striking animals play a vital role because they are more aggressive than horses and donkeys, and can scare away predators.[29] If you are lucky enough to drive across the state, chances are, somewhere along the miles of ranch land, you'll see at least one. Stay here in your mind for a moment. This zebra living among the herd of brown cows is like a lamp lighting up a dark room. An oddity living without inhibition, in striking contrast to her surroundings. Somehow, she knows, in her differences and separateness, there is nothing wrong with her or her presence there. It's beneficial. Her specific location is exactly where her master has designated her to be. She may look at odds with the others, sound peculiar, and even socialize in her distinct fashion, but it doesn't make her more or less than her bovine companions. The black and white beauty is confident in her striking appearance and knows how to wield it. Essentially, you can tell by watching, this zebra knows who she is and the purpose for which she lives. Therefore, she can go out into the center most part of the field, displaying the contrasts, the intricacies of her unique qualities, and the glory of her Maker. In a zebra manner, her Going and Showing while living out her normal days makes her unmistakable.

Consider the words of Jesus to be light in the darkness. Think about the zebra, where we find a bold contrast in a sea of sameness. Today is a good day to take a step forward and move away from the wall. If you will, consider yourself a zebra in the making. It's a visual that will help us remember the goal: to be visible. To keep the light on. To Go and Show.

Arise, shine, for your light has come, and the glory of the LORD rises upon you.

Isaiah 60:1 ESV

GOODBYE WALLFLOWER WAYS–

Buckle up, because the road to seen, heard, and known entails some of those failing forward exercises I mentioned, ensuring you can Go and Show confidently in your own vibrant beauty. The invitation remains. *Come into the light of the Savior.* You, too, supernaturally possess fetching stripes and resplendent contrasts, just like a bona fide zebra. And they are meant to be shown and shared. If you have Spotify or another entity where you find your music, listen to "Stand in Your Love."[30] We have too long been missing the likes of you.

DAY 19:
GREATER

We must show our Christian colors if we are to be true to
Jesus Christ.

~C. S. Lewis[31]

You might ask if we are on the right track. Is the proposal to "Go
and Show" too narcissistic for biblical Christianity? Too egomaniacal? Maybe the visibility suggested here is all too pompous and
self-centered? Could God's plan for your life and mine involve leaving shadow life to embrace a godly flamboyance in a crowd? Is it
reasonable and good to snub rejection and the dismissals from our
circles? Do we find the Word of God consistent with the concept of
being conspicuous and this portrayal of becoming the zebra?

If there ever lived a person in vibrant contrast to their environment
beyond Jesus, it was John the Baptist. In our search for a zebra amid
a herd of ordinary, John the Baptist is the créme de la créme. Isaiah
prophesied about someone coming before the Messiah as, "The voice
of one crying in the wilderness: 'Prepare the way of the Lord; make
his paths straight'" (Matthew 3:3 ESV). John's appearance was off
beat even by ancient standards. He spent his time in the wilderness
wearing clothing made of camel's hair with a leather belt tied around
it, eating a strange diet of locusts and honey (Matthew 3:4). From
the get-go, his mission on this planet was to embody a dissonance,
looking set apart, and bringing a distinctly different message.

The entire life and ministry of this John the Baptist hung on
his obedience to become the zebra, to Go and Show. He was to get
people ready for the coming Messiah, and this he did. Given the
Holy Spirit from before he was born (Luke 1:15), John recognized
who Jesus was (Luke 1:41, John 1:29-34), he spoke hard truths, and
did not shrink back or mince words when difficult conversations

were required (Luke 3:7). A baptism of people for repentance, not with the Holy Spirit (Matthew 3:11) was central to his ministry, preparing the way for the Savior. This unconventional man presented an unprecedented message. People came out in droves to hear John speak about the need to seek repentance and be baptized.

At the height of his ministry, when throngs of people followed John, Jesus turned up in the same area. John introduced Jesus to the crowds as, "the Lamb of God, who takes away the sins of the world!" (John 1:29 ESV), and in two shakes, John's followers turned away from their zebra to accompany this unknown phenomenon, the long-awaited Messiah. Suddenly the crowds diminished, and his awe-inspiring baptism numbers plummeted. People "unfollowed" John to run after this Jesus.

Upset by this impertinent and disloyal behavior, John's disciples questioned him. But John understood who he was. He was a solitary zebra planted in the mainstream of an ordinary cow pasture, responsible to help others find their way to this very Jesus. John was a man momentarily center stage getting all the attention, who rightly accepted Jesus overshadowing him in terms of importance, popularity, and prestige. John was not only content with this, but joyful about the development, reassuring his followers in the position of Jesus.

"He must increase, but I must decrease."

John 3:30 ESV

GOODBYE WALLFLOWER WAYS—

What do you think it looks like in your life for Jesus to become greater? John simply pointed people to the Truth rather than to himself. What might you need to do to take one step toward Jesus increasing and you decreasing?

Day 20:
The Grand Paradox

He must become greater and greater, and I must become less and less.

John 3:30 NLT

It is not long after the popularity reversal we talked about yesterday that authorities imprisoned John for doing exactly what he was supposed to be doing. King Herod swiped his brother's wife, Herodias, and married her himself. John the Baptist called the king out on this sinful move, along with other bad behaviors, and landed in a jail cell for his criticism (Luke 3:19-20).

So much for being "the voice of one calling 'make straight the paths,'" and getting the people ready for the coming Messiah. There is no heralding of good news when you are locked in a dungeon. No one can build a great ministry stuck in a corner, overlooked and forgotten. John finds himself in the dark, alone, far from a sense of fulfilling his calling, even questioning his ability to hear God (Luke 7:18-19). Letting his light shine and showing his stripes like a zebra left John the Baptist for dead in a dungeon.

What is going on here? There is a contradiction in the calling and experience of this man, John the Baptist, set apart for a purpose. He clearly has access to the secret handshake I believed existed for those like him. Here is a life littered with paradoxes, so much so that by the time John had been a captive in the miserable dungeon for a while, he questions whether he got anything right (Luke 7:19). Appointed to draw people to Truth, only to be silenced for it. Made a vibrant herald, bringing many to repentance, only to watch his ministry falter and wane on account of another. Called to make straight the paths, yet dismissed to a dungeon for his scrupulous work. He became lesser, so Jesus could become greater (John 3:30). These realities seemed so opposed, John questioned whether he could even hear God.

Before we move any further, we need to get something straight. Becoming seen is not altogether what you might think. John the Baptist enables us to recognize what zebra life is *not*. The focus is not vying for the front, accumulating likes, follows and shares. His front and center calling and his zebra-like vibrancy landed him with a death sentence in a dungeon. But there is no question, John's life was a solid win for eternity. When everything was on the line, our man, John, did not shrink back. He stood brazenly in who God made him to be, in all his exuberance, contrasting with his surroundings. Whether his followers were many or few, John spent his life pointing people to the Savior.

He must become greater. Lest you and I become disillusioned, before we can even begin Go and Show lessons, we need to understand who should dominate our pursuit. Frankly, it's not you. The life of John the Baptist illustrates how to Go and Show. Becoming seen is not so much about our reigning supreme through our social media outlets, but about Jesus becoming greater, and us becoming *unseen*. Here is the grand paradox. It's how we stand out like a zebra in a field of cows, and by what means we exit wallflower mode for good. Regardless of how others treat us, His becoming greater while we become lesser is the only true, joyful way to live as God intends.

But more than that, I count everything as loss compared to the priceless privilege and supreme advantage of knowing Christ Jesus my Lord [and of growing more deeply and thoroughly acquainted with Him—a joy unequaled]. For His sake I have lost everything, and I consider it all garbage, so that I may gain Christ,

Philippians 3:8 AMP

GOODBYE WALLFLOWER WAYS–

Write it. Circle it if you need to. Of prime importance to note on your successful plan toward a striking, purpose-filled Going and Showing is to *Make Him Greater*.

Day 21:
Change is Possible

Change happens not just by giving the mind new
arguments but also by feeding the imagination new
beauties.

~Timothy Keller[32]

John the Baptist is not the only one who demonstrates for us how
to Go and Show. If there was ever an example of someone who
transformed from being a card-carrying herd member to learning
how to develop his inner zebra, so to speak, in Going and Showing,
it was James. Seeing a zebra smack in the middle of a Texas hayfield is
a shock to the system for the first time. Though I suppose it's nothing
compared to the half-brother of Jesus encountering the resurrected
Savior face to face.

We know this happened according to Paul (1 Corinthians 15:7).
James did not stick his "Aha" moment in a drawer, writing it off
as a flash of delusion. We know this because he was there. James,
the brother of Jesus, was in the room when a mighty blast vibrated
through the entire structure from top to bottom (Acts 1:14, 2:1-
2). There was also the light. Everyone saw it and agreed. Although
unbelievable, the stories were the same. A single fire split and dispersed
out and onto each person in the shape of a tongue. That was the
Day of Pentecost, when the promised Holy Spirit descended upon
those gathered together. It was here James, along with Peter, John,
the brothers, James and Andrew, Philip and Thomas, Bartholomew
and Matthew, James, the son of Alphaeus, Simon the Zealot, Judas,
the son of James, a number of women, the mother of Jesus, and his
other brothers received the Holy Spirit in power (Acts 1:13-14, 2:4).

The question to ask is why James, the brother of Jesus, was present in the first place? James was a known skeptic of his brother. We might say he was a card-carrying member of the herd of ordinary. Many knew this. James irrefutably did not believe Jesus was the son of God. Crazy, maybe (Mark 3:21). Outlandish, somewhat deranged, a fruitcake, or a headcase, perhaps. Most definitely a character Johnny Depp would love to play. But this he knew: his brother was not the Messiah. For John tells us, ". . . not even his brothers believed in him," (John 7:5 ESV).

We know while He was alive, James was not on board with who Jesus declared Himself to be.[33] But the resurrection happened. Everything changed. What occurred, or the words uttered during the exchange, is unknown. What is known is the resurrected Jesus appeared to James, mano-a-mano, and he was never the same.

Then he appeared to more than five hundred brothers at one time, most of whom are still alive, though some have fallen asleep. Then he appeared to James, then to all the apostles.

1 Corinthians 15:6-7 ESV

That's the impact Jesus can have on a life even today. When Jesus enters your life, you are never the same. With Jesus, change is possible. To see what I mean and precisely how it can play out today, in your life, stay on track. There was a reason James was in that room that particular day, and it changed him forever. There is a reason you are here, reading about it today.

Therefore we do not become discouraged [spiritless, disappointed, or afraid]. Though our outer self is [progressively] wasting away, yet our inner self is being [progressively] renewed day by day.

2 Corinthians 4:16 AMP

GOODBYE WALLFLOWER WAYS—

If you are honest, unlimited by resources, time, and space, what about your life would you want Jesus to change? Now the more personal question: What about *yourself* would you want Him to change?

DAY 22:
A RESURRECTED JESUS ENCOUNTER

All these with one accord were devoting themselves to prayer,
together with the women and Mary the mother of Jesus, and
his brothers.

Acts 1:14 ESV

What happened to James is similar to Hagar's encounter. An unbelieving nobody, insignificant in anyone else's eyes, is pursued, seen, and found. Like our servant girl throwaway, Jesus saw James, the dissenting brother, and came for him full force. The resurrected Jesus gave James a face-to-face reunion. This unmistakable confrontation with Truth against all the religion this good Jewish boy held dear led to a radical and stupefying upset.

Scripture illuminates the change by making sure we notice James is present when the Holy Spirit lands on the room gathered in prayer on the Day of Pentecost (Acts 1:14). Waiting for the promised Helper to arrive, this brother prays with the other followers of Jesus. Anticipating the next move by the one true Savior who was his very own brother. James lived with Him up close and personal, yet missed seeing Him for who and what He was his entire life. For thirty years, he looked toward the herd rather than toward Jesus. Not again. After James encountered Jesus resurrected, he was never the same.

James moves from ordinary herd member to remarkable zebra, from skeptic heckler to leading the church in Jerusalem (Acts 21:18). This man became a trusted confidant of Paul (Galatians 1:18-19), so integral to the Christian movement that by the time Peter is imprisoned (Acts 12) and miraculously freed by an angel, Peter instructs those gathered together praying for his release to tell

James, specifically, and then the apostles (Acts 12:17). James rose to such prominence he became the leader of the Jewish Christians in Jerusalem. He remained in that position until, according to church history, he was told by Jewish authorities to recant Jesus or be thrown off the pinnacle of the Temple to his death.[34]

Was this narcissism run amuck? Or was James a conspicuous reflection of who he knew Jesus to be?

James chose to Go and Show to his death. That is the mark of the power of the Gospel. Jesus is the driving force who enables you to move from your invisible life to wholly significant. He makes the replaceable indispensable, the worthless essential, and those who have remained unseen to be revealed. James exemplifies what it's like to blend in with the ordinary until he encounters the risen Jesus. From that moment, the half-brother of Jesus launched on a trajectory toward zebra-ness that lasted until his dying breath. James stood out, courageously unmoved in his faith to the end. His lamp was lit and could not be hidden, even with those in power trying to cover it up. His stripes were unhidden and his stance immovable.

I have been crucified with Christ. It is no longer I who live, but Christ who lives in me. And the life I now live in the flesh I live by faith in the Son of God, who loved me and gave himself for me.

Galatians 2:20 ESV

GOODBYE WALLFLOWER WAYS—

Consider what you have learned about the transformation in James. What strikes you most about who he was before and after his resurrected Jesus encounter?

DAY 23:
SEEING WHAT'S REALLY REAL

The question is not what you look at, but what you see.

~Robert D. Richardson, Jr.[35]

Gazing at a zebra as a whole can create an optical illusion. Is the animal white with black stripes or black with white stripes? At a glance, most assume zebras are white with black stripes because of their white underbellies. Genetics has demystified the age-old quandary.[36] Pigmentation or the lack thereof makes the stripes. The skin is actually dark under their fur. Stripes are created by "pigment inhibition," or the absence of pigment in certain areas of the coat.[37] White stripes appear on the black skin where there is no pigmentation present. When you and I look at a zebra and see a white underbelly and organized white stripes, we are not *seeing* what's really real. We think we see white with black stripes when, in actuality, the opposite is true.

Why so much ado about zebras? James thought he saw what most did after all those years of being a good Jewish man. The Law of Moses was the way to God, and his brother, Jesus, was nothing but cuckoo. It was like seeing black stripes on a white body. But he was wrong. It took a personal encounter of epic proportions to help James see what was really real, much like recognizing the coloring on a zebra.

For so many years, I held beliefs that were not true—moments and messages from my experiences that I believed were truths in the Bible. I took my treatment by others as my worth. I gave credence to the criticisms. I held tightly to the wallpaper because I reckoned it was the only place for me. But I was wrong. I was as wrong as

James denying his brother's deity to His face. In a sense, I was seeing black stripes on a white body. For me, recognizing the truth wasn't a once and done experience. Mine was a long series of believing and conscious choosings to see white stripes on a black body.

Only God clears the blinding fog of bad theology and optical illusions so entrenched in our hearts and minds. He alone can give eyes to see what's really real. Isaiah tells us, ". . . the eyes of the blind shall be opened, and the ears of the deaf unstopped" (Isaiah 35:5 ESV).

Even Paul prays for those entrusted to him, that the eyes of their hearts will be enlightened, so they will know "the hope of His calling, what are the riches of the glory of His inheritance in the saints" (Ephesians 1:18 NKJV). It's what God has done in my own life and what He wants to do in your life as well.

Open my eyes to see the wonderful truths in your instructions.

Psalm 119:18 NLT

GOODBYE WALLFLOWER WAYS—

Today, I pray God will begin clearing away what blinds you, giving you the ability to hear well and see what's really real.

DAY 24:
EMBRACE YOUR SPACE

We often don't realize that where God puts us is the very place we need to be to receive what He wants to give us.

~Priscilla Shirer[38]

Where has God placed you? James, as a disciple of Jesus, understood the location God placed him in to be strategic, and he embraced it full throttle. His setting wasn't hiding in a cave, practicing silence, or holding small group sessions in secret, although it might be for some. His place was city center, where the opposition was fierce and the needs were great. James led the Christian church in the middle of unspeakable violence, poverty, and certain persecution. But not everyone sees white stripes, choosing to embrace where God places them.

Take the tribe of Joseph. Long before James came on the scene, the tribe of Joseph (Ephraim and Manasseh) was one of the twelve tribes who came out of Egypt in anticipation of receiving an inheritance in the Promised Land. Years went by. Moses died, and Joshua led the people into taking Jericho and several other areas. The tribe of Joseph remained without their personal space. Don't think for a minute God had slighted them. They had not followed through on the instructions. God gave word to Joshua to divide out the land based on the size of the tribes. He settled boundaries. Victories were declared. But the actual conquering was still to be done by each tribe, to take possession of what they had already received.

A city known as Gezer was a part of the territory allotted for the tribe of Joseph (Joshua 16:5-10). This city was important, not because of its size or resources, but because of its strategic location for trade routes. Situated fifteen miles outside Jerusalem, Gezer flanked a super highway for trade in those days along the Mediterranean Sea, as well as an essential path toward Jerusalem.[39] On the one hand, you could have viewed Gezer as a perfect location, filled with life and the pulse of the culture. On the other, we could see it as a gosh-awful place no one would ever choose to live because of all the people moving through it and the constant hustle.

Certainly, if you wanted to make an impact in the area, Gezer would be essential. Whoever possessed this city would have a significant influence over the territory and beyond. It's easy to see God's aim is often different from ours. He gave His people the prime location of Gezer on purpose for the extending of His Name and glory to the entire area, but they didn't see it. And they never fully possessed it.

However, they did not drive out the Canaanites who lived in Gezer, so the Canaanites have lived in the midst of Ephraim to this day but have been made to do forced labor.

Joshua 16:10 ESV

Not a lot has changed through the generations. This remains God's aim. He's not trying to keep His people holed up in small comfortable spaces where it's easy and acceptable to be a Christian. God is on mission with us. Still. He is strategic about *location*.

And he made from one man every nation of mankind to live on all the face of the earth, having determined allotted periods and the boundaries of their dwelling place.

Acts 17:26 ESV

He means you and me to be right where He has planted us—in our neighborhoods, in our work relationships, in our churches, and wherever else we might find ourselves. I'm not talking about abusive situations or giving the impression it's good and right to ride life out being surrounded by comfortable. Maybe it's uncomfortable. It could even be hostile. Instead of complaining, trying to get out of it, or running away from our herd into the corner under a nice tree of respite somewhere, consider your locale calculated.

> *The steps of a man are established by the LORD, when he delights in his way; though he fall, he shall not be cast headlong, for the LORD upholds his hand.*

Psalm 37:23-24 ESV

GOODBYE WALLFLOWER WAYS—

What if God has been strategic in his placement of you? No one has access to your sphere of influence like you. Imagine what might happen if you and I committed to accepting God's sovereignty in where we are by embracing our God-given space, showing our stripes as we go. What is one specific way you can embrace the space God has given?

DAY 25:
SEEING WHITE STRIPES

The absence of God in most spheres of life is perceived
to be normal, and even Christians feel it as normal—
which is why absorbing the culture all around us and its
priorities is so dangerous.

~John Piper[40]

When you know a zebra is black with white stripes, it's hard to see them as anything else anymore. Our friend, James, once a part of the herd, turned zebra, never saw black stripes again. He only saw white. Jesus changed everything from the inside out.

After years of service, James wrote a letter we know as the book of James in the Bible. In those pages, he beckons the reader to *see* differently, like himself, so they can *live* differently. There is not a better biblical pattern for learning how to leave this sense of invisibility—to Go and Show—than what we have from this man. Not only did he experience a radical transformation, but he also remained in and among his herd. James didn't back down, cower, or look for an easier way to quietly love Jesus. He did not resort to wallflower status. When temptation to conform would have been great, he resisted.

James demonstrates how to choose significance over popularity. We learn from his refreshing example how to embrace the person God designed us to be when the majority may not agree. He models how to stand out resolute where God places us, even when it's in the middle of naysayers. Shameless and confident, armed with courage, and full of faith.

Faith in Jesus was real to James. Jesus as the Savior of the world was worth standing out against all his cultural sameness demanded. Still, he recognized there was more to Going and Showing than a mere desire to be different. It was more than half-hearted efforts and want-to's. It exceeded my cute t-shirt, spotty church attendance, and social media posts.

> *And let steadfastness have its full effect, that you may be perfect and complete, lacking in nothing.*
>
> James 1:4 ESV

We can't wing it to "perfect and complete." Not only do we need to look to Jesus, like James, we need a new way of seeing. The best way to get from here to there is to look intently at one who has gone before us. For the rest of this journey, James will lead the way. Remarkable to note how his letter closely resembles the words of Jesus from the Sermon on the Mount,[41] and it's loaded with practicality. Oh, it's not the only place we will investigate, but you will finish your days relating well to a fellow zebra, knowing he showed you how to see differently, moving you out of the shadows into the light of the Savior.

> *Have nothing to do with irreverent, silly myths. Rather train yourself for godliness;*
>
> 1 Timothy 4:7

GOODBYE WALLFLOWER WAYS—

Think about all you have already learned. Up to this point in your journey, has your thinking changed? What is different about your perspective on Day 25 compared to Day 1?

Day 26:
Failing Forward Feat #3

Knowing who we are in Christ sets us free from the
need to impress others.

~Joyce Meyer[42]

What Paul writes in Ephesians 1:3-14 did more to move me out of the shadows than anything else. Why? Because it blew up my suitcase. In this passage, you will find at least ten to twelve gifts God has given to every believer in Christ. These are not privileges and blessings reserved for the few, requiring the special handshake or seminary degree. They are for you, my friend. They are also for any of us hard-headed, disbelieving chicks quick to run to the curtains and slow to recognize the blessings.

Your adventure is to read this passage. List the ten to twelve privileges and blessings Paul articulates are ours in Christ. Keep these handy, because you are going to need them sooner rather than later.

PART II
CHAPTER 4

HOW TO BECOME VISIBLE

Praise God, we can change. True transformation begins as you and I behold and then grasp hold of elements a person seen and intimately known by God needs to perceive as reality. It was in these discoveries I really began to live beyond the shadows cast upon me by others, myself, and my circumstances. In essence, these are the very fundamentals every wallflower needs to apprehend to become visible.

DAY 27:
YOUR CALLING

Use me, God. Show me how to take who I am, who I want
to be, and what I can do, and use it for a purpose greater
than myself.

~Martin Luther King, Jr.[43]

Childhood recess can leave a mark. Where I grew up, unless your
teeth were in jeopardy, or you broke a bone, the adults didn't pay
attention to fairness, feelings, or failings. It was the kind of environment where thicker skins developed and existing hurts became more
ingrained. Exclusion from a game with the popular girls, vicious
name calling, or the humiliation of being the last resort when teams
divided could be painful pricks, especially when reinforced through
the years. Maybe you can relate. Maybe you still feel those pinpricks
as you replay the memories. The dread of recognizing all you are not
can be debilitating to the point we find ourselves in the corner, once
again, questioning God's purpose for our lives.

From the opening lines of his book, if ever he was like me, James
left all that dread on the playground. In one sentence, the man-
turned-zebra declared his clear sense of God's purpose for his life.

*James, a servant of God and of the Lord Jesus Christ, to the
twelve tribes in the Dispersion: Greetings.*

James 1:1 ESV

The victory is not making a smart choice about whether to become a plumber as opposed to the expected carpenter, but knowing to whom he belongs and how that should play out in his life. Paul describes this knowing to the Corinthians, asking them to consider who God calls. He writes, "God chose what is low and despised in the world, even the things that are not, to bring to nothing the things that are, so that no human being might boast in the presence of God. And because of him you are in Christ Jesus, who became to us wisdom from God, righteousness and sanctification and redemption" (1 Corinthians 1:28-30 ESV). These individuals lean toward obscurity. Here Paul rightly reminds them of God's strange work of the Gospel in them so that Jesus might get the glory, rather than man.

You can see the potential problems if we were left in charge. The prettiest people would get the gifts and blessings. The smartest would be privy to the truth. Leaders would bully the rest of us into submission to follow. We would reserve all other offices for the wealthy. My super-secret Christian club would come together in two shakes, leaving the rest of humanity out of luck.

Thankfully, it's not my Gospel. It's not the Gospel Paul preaches, nor the one James writes about. God chooses the weak, those with no pedigree, who are unworthy of notice. Non-essentials. The nothings of this world. He chooses them on purpose. There is room for you and for me.

What is your calling, my friend?

Has God found you in all your obscurity, like James? Your God specializes in calling the things that are not, as if they are. He already has big plans for you.

Each of you should use whatever gift you have received to serve others, as faithful stewards of God's grace in its various forms. if anyone speaks, they should do so as one who speaks the very words of God. If anyone serves, they should do so with the strength God provides, so that in all things God may be praised through Jesus Christ. To him be the glory and the power for ever and ever. Amen.

1 Peter 4:10-11 NIV

BECOMING VISIBLE—

Although James holds a place of prominence, leading the Christian church in Jerusalem, he calls himself the servant of God and Jesus Christ. What if you took on this same calling? Consider one difference you could make today toward this goal.

Day 28:
What You Cannot See

It's a big world. Don't get trapped by tiny dreams and feeble problems. Time for big prayers and bold faith.

~Louie Giglio[44]

Not long ago, my husband made a vocational pivot. We expected a lateral move in the same town within the current school district, keeping everything familiar. Instead, Chad packed a trailer and rented an apartment in a major city hours away. A year later, we sold our forever home, packed up our enormous family, re-homed the dog, and the kids and I left familiar behind to join him.

Imagine a child forced to eat liver and onions for a month. That sums up our feelings on the move. Yuck. We questioned why anyone would choose to live in such a muggy, traffic-jammed, fast-paced, seemingly God-forsaken place. What was the Lord thinking sending us somewhere so awful? For heaven's sake, has He seen the traffic? The crime? The unfriendly non-Southernness of the massive metro area?

Still, we watched God work amazing wonders across the details. Yes, we were going to be part of the misguided 6.2 million, traffic and all. And the journey getting there was nothing short of frustrating.

Running a household with eight kids is challenging even for a mom and dad team. Take away half the players and it can fall apart before half-time. While my spouse was away that first year, all sorts of small spontaneous disasters occurred. If it could break, it broke. From flooding kitchens and flat tires to ER visits, personal stalkers, and animals dying, the time was hard on all fronts.

It was a season of daily exercises in trusting God for what I could not see. Any time I was in distress, He met my need. My husband would unexpectedly get to come home, or my father-in-law would call me, saying, "Cheri, I just had a feeling you might need something." Indeed, I did. Men from our Sunday School class patrolled the neighborhood to keep watch on the stalker until he was stopped. On all fronts, God showed up.

Joshua experienced his own trying season of God meeting his needs in the nick of time. Within a few years of crossing the Jordan, he fought and defeated thirty-one kings in the Promised Land (Joshua 12). But he didn't allow himself to get comfortable in the familiar. God was still on the move. Age did not matter. Past accomplishments did not grant permission for retirement. In the very next verses, God instructs him that "there remains yet very much land to possess" (Joshua 13:1 ESV).

This is no time to settle in for observing and sideline living. Familiar is no place for you. Forget your birthdate. Older or younger, a vast territory remains at stake.

Like me, you may have difficulty seeing beyond the crisis at hand. Regardless of the future, consider your experiences that which God uses to show Himself faithful, to move you beyond familiar.

Let your work be shown to your servants,

and your glorious power to their children.

Let the favor of the Lord our God be upon us,

and establish the work of our hands upon us;

yes, establish the work of our hands!

Psalm 90:16-17 ESV

BECOMING VISIBLE—

Add Psalm 90:16-17 to your everyday prayer list and begin praying it over your own life. Celebrate this reality. God wants to use your life in ways you cannot yet perceive.

DAY 29:
LOSE YOUR CIRCLE; FIND YOUR TRIBE

Being consumed by what people think of you is the fastest
way to forget what God thinks of you.

~Craig Groeschel[45]

My sister has five best friends. What about you?

Me neither. Most of us are hoping for two or three women to like us.[46] People who embrace us with our make-up off and our worst attitudes on. Too often, we push our wants and wishes aside to settle for simply being accepted into the herd of ordinary. But this method of relationship gaining can be exhausting.

We perform a medley of shenanigans to gain their approval, like adopting hobbies we hate, spending money we would rather keep, and talking about things we don't enjoy. We knock ourselves out being who they want us to be, doing what they want us to do.

My winding path has taught me that craving to be liked and to have a few close friends is not the problem. It's where and how I am trying to achieve it.

*There's trouble ahead when you live only for the approval of
others, saying what flatters them, doing what indulges them.
Popularity contests are not truth contests—look how many
scoundrel preachers were approved by your ancestors! Your
task is to be true, not popular.*

Luke 6:26 THE MESSAGE

In your quest for Going and Showing, know that God has more for you than succumbing to that old, comfortable sameness. He desires more for you than herd dependence.

Experts suggest we operate with an emotional capacity of one hundred and fifty social connections.[47] Picture a target with the ring closest to the bullseye representing your dearest relationships. That's where my sister has an overload and you and I feel a deficit. Only about five people should fit here, inclusive of your dearest people. The next ring holds fifteen people (co-workers, relatives, and friends) who are important to you outside the inner circle. Fifty more friends of friends, like acquaintances, fill in the next ring. These are not the people you share your dirty dirt with. Beyond this ring lie meaningful contacts, but you don't know them well enough to pick their cousin up from the airport.[48]

Think about your own relationships and where certain people might land within the rings on the target. For those of us looking at our inner one or two circles, feeling pains of emptiness, remnants of exhaustion, and the scars of repeated rejection—consider, it might be time to lose your circle. Sometimes we move people into circles where they have no rightful place.

I'm not suggesting you divorce anyone or hang up on your long-time frenemy from high school because you can. This is not permission to go rogue. Do cease striving after what will never be. There are people who will like you and need you as much as you need them. Keep in mind, Going and Showing where God places you often requires loss.

Find your tribe. Relax. You don't need twenty besties. Just one or two God-honoring loyal and lasting souls.

Walk with the wise and become wise, for a companion of fools suffers harm.

Proverbs 13:20 NIV

BECOMING VISIBLE—

Ask God to orchestrate and build your relationships. Sometimes they are already present. Seek His wisdom to recognize people with whom to build stronger ties for His glory and your good. He is The Giving God.

DAY 30:
DIFFERENT AS GOOD

So it stands to reason that as we are filled with Him, we will reflect His holiness and purity in who we are, in what we say, and in what we do. As a result, our lives will be in sharp contrast to those around us.

~Anne Graham Lotz[49]

Suppose you spend five, maybe ten years trying to assimilate into a group. You invest in your circles, but the relationships feel one-sided. After participating and engaging with your surroundings, after all that time and energy you put in, you still gel with your circle of friends like oil and water.

Is it you?

Not in the sense that something is wrong with you. We've been through all that. Zebras don't blend well with a sea of ordinary Hereford red. Instead, a one-time wallflower who is becoming a zebra is likely to cause some bristling and may draw out the ugly. That doesn't make her a problem. Different is good in this context.

But, yes, it is you, if you are looking toward the herd for approval. (I'm beating the topic with a stick because, well…it's sticky.) We find it elsewhere in the Bible. Paul encourages the Roman believers not to entrust themselves to others or to assimilate into the culture.

Don't copy the behavior and customs of this world, but let
God transform you into a new person by changing the way

you think. Then you will learn to know God's will for you,
which is good and pleasing and perfect.

Romans 12:2 NLT

I admit, the desire lingers. For years, I clung to the herd, caring too much about what others thought. This was especially prevalent for me in Christian environments. What John states about the authorities in the days of Jesus (John 12:42-43) was true about me. I stayed hidden, trying to blend into the Hereford lot because I loved the glory that comes from man more than the glory that comes from God.

By the time James is writing, other people's opinions hold no power over him. Why not? Why doesn't this man care what other people think? While Jesus walked the planet, James served as an outspoken poster child for the Jewish cause. Don't you suppose his nearest and dearest snubbed his newfound longings? Can't you imagine he lost his circle somewhere in the transformation?

Likely. Yet, at some point, James recognizes being *a servant of God and of the Lord Jesus* means embracing God's opinion above that of anyone else. We cannot find our worth in our social media personas, the success of our spouse, our bank accounts, the letters following our name, how well our children turn out, or the brand of purse we carry. Letting go of the death grip hold of what other people think of us is nothing short of essential. The ruts in my trail of failing forward are deep on this particular road. I've thrown a lot of mud in this area of my fence, trying to get the truth on the matter to stick and forge a way ahead. Allow me to pass my worn notes back.

At the top of the page, find these instructions: *Stop participating.*

I made these mental notes for myself when a popular girl in my circle approached me with a mouthful of disapproval for something I finally came to recognize as catty and insignificant. I did not do what she wanted, when we never agreed I would. When she finished sufficiently giving me the what for, she flipped around and marched off to her besties, leaving me to bask in her emotional emissions.

My normal response was to apologize for not yielding to her demands, crumbling emotionally, then invisibly slinking to my corner. Alone. But not this time. In the middle of her tirade, I had an epiphany: *I am a high school graduate.* I did not need to succumb to the whims and wants of the prom queen of yesteryear just because she had conditioned others well into adulthood. As I listened, unmoved by her tantrum, I finished my lemonade. I did not meet her demands. The response she hoped for fell flat. I did not cower or apologize for upsetting her applecart. The most influential person in my circle had no hold on me. Finally. It still hurt, but not participating was liberating. And it has led to many other similar victories.

> *Leave the presence of a fool, for there you do not meet words of knowledge.*
>
> Proverbs 14:7 ESV

BECOMING VISIBLE—

Leave the drama packed up with your cap and gown. You have permission not to take part in the same old power games. Just don't do it. In this one way, your life will demonstrate a love for the glory of God over man.

Day 31:
Joy in God

For there exists a delight that is not given to the wicked,
but to those honoring Thee, O God, without desiring
recompense, the joy of whom Thou art Thyself!

~Aurelius Augustine[50]

Delighting in God? Honestly, I feel like that's one of those connections reserved for the Super Spiritual Club. Why? Because it sounds *super spiritual*. That's what I thought until it turned up while reading that One Year Bible.

Amid historical obscurity, something peculiar popped out of the monotony of dos and don'ts. I noticed every year God required the Israelites to gather before Him for three feasts. They were to feast for seven days, "because the LORD your God will bless you in all your produce and in all the work of your hands, so that you will be altogether joyful" (Deuteronomy 16:15 ESV).

Rejoicing before the Lord was the mandatory expectation. Like spending holidays with your Great Aunt Louise who insists you eat her "famous" meatballs, the Bible leaves no room for side-stepping. Unlike your aunt's cuisine, perhaps, this obligatory rejoicing was no drudgery because there was promise built into the request. God would knock their socks off in terms of productivity. They would relish the opportunity to rejoice in Him, bursting with happiness because of all God's blessings upon them. And everyone would hear about it. It was a perfect arrangement. It would glorify God through their rejoicing in His gifts.

The New Testament explains joy in God much the same way. Joy is not bound to earthly blessings, like crops and land productivity, but in what will last through eternity.

These things I have spoken to you, that my joy may be in you, and that your joy may be full.

John 15:11 ESV

To find joy in God is just what zebras do. We see this in the life and experience of Blaise Pascal, who caught sight of this joy and was never the same. On November 23, 1654, he had what he describes as "a Divine encounter" with the one true God, and had a reminder of the event sewn into his jacket as a declaration of his own conversion. On it he wrote "Joy, joy, joy, tears of joy."[51] Joy unexplainable. To Pascal, that was the defining factor. Delight in God he had never experienced.

So what's the big deal about joy for someone wanting to be seen?

No joy—no zebra.

Suppose we could step back in time for one of the three feasts. But instead of rejoicing in God for all He has done, we think about our exceptional equipment, or the neighbors who helped bring in the crops. Suppose a new method of farming yielded a lot more produce than before? Pretty soon, we rejoice in our knowledge, the friends who helped us, or progress. But God? There is no joy in Him.

Joy results when you and I embrace who God is, recognizing the impact He has on our lives. It's a divine work. That kind of delight cannot be hidden. Not even in the inside panel of a jacket.

Be gracious to me, O Lord, for to you do I cry all the day. Gladden the soul of your servant, for to you, O Lord, do I lift up my soul.

Psalm 86:3-4 ESV

BECOMING VISIBLE—

I invite you to pray Psalm 86:3-4 every day until it becomes a reality in your life.

DAY 32:
JOY IN BADNESS

Count it all joy, my brothers, when you meet trials of various kinds, for you know that the testing of your faith produces steadfastness.

James 1:2-3 ESV

The book of James oozes with practicality in how to walk out your faith in daily life. It's not a comfortable read, but a field manual in how you, too, can be the zebra you never imagined. Leave shadow living and unproductive namby-pamby Christianity (2 Timothy 3:5) to pursue a life lacking in nothing.

The first stop is joy. Joy in the middle of badness.

Wait. What about joy in God? Isn't that enough? Must I be happy about my problems? Why can't I suffer through it, gritting my teeth and taking my licks? Maybe I will stay depressed for long periods of time. Hold on to my anger, letting it ooze into my relationships. Remain the victim. What's wrong with all that? People do it all the time. Why can't we just walk out the badness as terrible?

James calls us to something radically different. First, to experience joy when we meet trials of various kinds is not joy despite badness. We're not commanded to put on a cheerful face or that there is something deeply wrong with us when we can't. Troubles and difficulties of any kind are still, well, bad.

Instead, it's a joy *by way of the badness*. This response is a joy arising within us because of the difficulty. It's a joy working though the sorrow, like strength coming out of weakness, or when we see God bringing life out of death. A tremendous paradox, but purely impossible. We find this call to joy out of difficulty with Paul in Romans (Romans 5:3-5) with Peter echoing the same sentiment (1 Peter 1:6-7). These guys recognize the Christian life as more than unicorns and candy corn, experiencing God's divine work of joy through difficulties.

James knows perfection will not come holed up in the shadows. I'm sorry. *Perfect and complete* does not occur without problems, failures, and disappointments in the mix. And his audience would hear his words remembering Abraham's testing (Genesis 22:1) that brought an eternal reward for his perseverance. They would be familiar with Job's trials and vindication. And although the very idea of rejoicing under trials smacks us in the face with pure ridiculousness, scholars believe the structure reads like a traditional saying that would have circulated in the early church, not original to James.[52] Rejoicing during trials because it works toward your good in becoming who Jesus longs for you to be may be ear piercing news to you and me, but to the original audience, it was like the refrain of Amazing Grace—a timely reminder.

Embracing joy because of your difficulties, as only God can orchestrate in your life, is a Going and Showing event like none other. We don't need unicorns. Just joy.

*We can rejoice, too, when we run into problems and trials,
for we know that they help us develop endurance. And
endurance develops strength of character, and character
strengthens our confident hope of salvation. And this hope
will not lead to disappointment. For we know how dearly
God loves us, because he has given us the Holy Spirit to fill
our hearts with his love.*

Romans 5:3-5 NLT

BECOMING VISIBLE—

Tuck James 1:2-3 and Romans 5:3-5 into your bank of resources as you ask Jesus to help infuse joy into any trouble, difficulty or problem you encounter. He is the only one who can.

Day 33:
Get Your Theology Straight

Our minds may be like some computers that can have a
lifetime of wrong information stored in them.

~Joyce Meyer[53]

There we were, at the Empire State Building. Chad and I escaped without our entourage to New York on an anniversary trip. Images tucked away all my life about where we stood rushed to the front of my mind. Scenes from *Sleepless in Seattle* overran the crowded room. But then the romance of the moment fell away. Fantasy dissipated into the old, urban-legend fear some nine-year-old hooligan might yank a penny from his pocket to drop off the building. (You know, that would annihilate some innocent bystander on the sidewalk below.)

We know the death-penny fear like we know not to swim for thirty minutes after eating. Why? We're not sure. But for the love of all things good, just don't do it! Those who came before us forged the path in the necessities of life, such as the dangers of high-velocity pennies and how to avoid . . . I don't know what in a swimming pool. Leg cramps? I'm dubious. Yet you and I adopt these cautionary tales from our childhoods as Gospel truth.

Shocking as it was to learn, *Mythbusters* debunked the penny phobia.[54] We can forever roam the sidewalks along the foundation of the Empire State Building carefree. And there is no documented benefit for waiting half an hour for the swimming bit,[55] except maybe parents aren't ready to go.

Sometimes we get it wrong. We believe statements that aren't true because we have heard them enough times.[56] Take, for instance, "I know God won't give me more than I can handle. I just wish He didn't trust me so much." Yeah, you've heard it, too. We like to put this truism on the wall or on social media. It sounds virtuous. It appears biblical. Mother Teresa is the favored author, and if so, she got it wrong.[57] It's not biblical. Not even close. God will absolutely give you more than you can handle. Just ask Paul.

> *For we do not want you to be unaware, brothers, of the affliction we experienced in Asia. For we were so utterly burdened beyond our strength that we despaired of life itself.*
>
> 2 Corinthians 1:8 ESV

In moving beyond unhappy amid trouble, we need to stop telling ourselves something is wrong with us because we can't get a grip. If you are thinking, *God thinks I can do it or He would not have given it to me. What's wrong with me?* It's your theology. That's what's wrong.

James calls us to do something superhuman. We cannot turn our unhappy into joy solo. Paul continues:

> *Indeed, we felt that we had received the sentence of death. But that was to make us rely not on ourselves but on God who raises the dead.*
>
> 2 Corinthians 1:9 ESV

Handling your difficulty—giving you the power to rejoice through your suffering—is what God does. We should expect too much to handle—the amount that leaves us needy and dependent on a God who can raise dead people. Girl, you cannot handle your heartache, the loss, the cancer, the rejection, the stress—whatever your tough season looks like. He does not trust you to do it on your own. You are going to break.

Drop a penny from any building on the planet. You're good. Eat a sandwich in the pool while you doggy paddle. But never, not once, ever, believe you can handle your difficult situation alone.

Get your theology straight. Straight from the Bible, not a plague or a post, a person, or a devotional. Your need is to make you rely on the One who raises the dead. Praise God. That. Is. Not. You.

Now may the God of peace who brought again from the dead our Lord Jesus, the great shepherd of the sheep, by the blood of the eternal covenant, equip you with everything good that you may do his will, working in us that which is pleasing in his sight, through Jesus Christ, to whom be glory forever and ever. Amen.

Hebrews 13:20-21 ESV

BECOMING VISIBLE—

Add Hebrews 13:20-21 to memory. He is the God who raises the dead and equips you with all you need to do what He calls you to do.

DAY 34:
SLEEP STANDING

For as the body apart from the spirit is dead, so also faith apart from works is dead.

James 2:26 ESV

I prefer big dogs. The larger and hairier, the better. Currently, we have two French Bouvier mixed with some Great White Pyrenees. These breeds weigh around a hundred pounds with fur grown out eight or ten inches from head to toe. Max and Lola are basically oversized walking carpets. I chose them for their lounging personalities, the fur, of course, but primarily their protective natures.

An attempted break in years ago while I was alone in the house introduced life with canine giants in the mix. My spouse rescued two English Mastiffs and before this night, I wasn't a fan. There was a lot of drooling and passing gas in the togetherness and I had no mind to keep them. All the negatives became water under the bridge and they found a new home when those two alerted me to the danger in time to secure the perimeter and set the alarms. Moments later, the alarms went off because someone or something entered unwelcomed. The police arrived, determining someone had penetrated the property, and we've had big protective dogs ever since.

What I love about my portable rugs, Max and Lola, like their predecessors, is their keen awareness of friend versus foe. I belong in the house. The Amazon man does not. Before I even know he has arrived, Lola is staring him down through the window. Max is helping, vocally defending his turf. But all is quiet when their people return from school or work. No threats detected. They can rest easy.

Zebras are a lot like my big dogs. They migrate in the savanna freely with thousands of wildebeest yearly because of their keen senses. Zebras are more vigilant than wildebeest, with special skills designed to protect the herds. The placement of their eyes makes it possible to scan for predators even while they are grazing.[58] They also use a vocal warning system to communicate with others the potential dangers. But my favorite God-given feature is that zebras sleep standing.

I share these random facts about dogs and zebras because we find each doing what they were created to do, regardless of the cost. The Amazon man will not miss Max standing at the front door. Protecting is what God made him to do. Zebras sleep standing by design. And you and I were made to Go and Show our faith in what we do and say, day in and day out. Charles Spurgeon wrote:

A man who can keep his godliness to himself, has so small a proportion of it, I am afraid it will be no credit to himself, and no blessing to other people.[59]

If you profess to be a Jesus lover, but make your faith a private matter, you might as well remain in the shadows. When there is no evidence of transformation in your life, your faith is dead.

Whoever confesses that Jesus is the Son of God, God abides in him, and he in God.

1 John 4:15 ESV

BECOMING VISIBLE—

Has there been a time in your life when you know you have confessed your sin before God, trusting Jesus with your life? ". . .

If you confess with your mouth that Jesus is Lord and believe in your heart that God raised him from the dead, you will be saved" (Romans 10:9 ESV). Today, you can make this your reality. You can pray, "I confess my sin and believe You forgive me. And because Jesus paid for my sin, I will be saved from this moment on. Thank You for this gift of grace and mercy," believing that He can and He will, and you will be saved.

If you made this decision today, myself and my team at She Yearns Ministries, want to follow up with you to encourage you and help you follow Jesus beyond this book. Contact us at info@sheyearns.com and let us celebrate with you and help you get connected with others in your local area.

Day 35:
Do What is Unnatural

Here I stand. I can do no other. God help me. Amen.

~Martin Luther[60]

Our daughter Jolee came to us with a hole in her heart. An Atrial Septal Defect (or ASD)—a condition we felt we could manage. Chad and I have five college degrees between us, and he is a board-certified medical doctor in two fields of medicine. A heart defect with medical complications we could handle. A child with too many unidentifiable developmental and psychological issues to diagnose or treat (which became our reality overnight) left our family fractured. And I questioned the future. It was as if a torrential rain storm settled over my life that never let up, giving little visibility and formidable conditions for going anywhere. This gloomy outlook colored my thoughts, hopes, and even my prayers.

The Lord had given me more than I could handle, so to Him I went. My prayer was that He fix the broken. Surely the One who raises the dead can make my daughter well. I mean, He led us to her and made the way possible, He can lead us to solutions. Right diagnosis. Therapy and medicines to remedy what's wrong. God knows I am not equipped to deal with anything less. In my right trusting, God spoke through His Word.

For the LORD your God is living among you. He is a mighty savior. He will take delight in you with gladness. With his love, he will calm all your fears. He will rejoice over you with joyful songs.

Zephaniah 3:17 NLT

There is promise here. Absolutely. Personal assurance that God is not looking in on my situation from a distance. He is present in it. God can and does save. He does so, not because we deserve it or because we ask, but because He delights in you and in me, personally. All the unknowns and pieces that no longer fit together in my life are not obstacles. He calms all my fears. All of them. I don't need to worry about turning my unhappy into anything. The Lord Himself rejoices over me in my mixed-up fearful brokenness with joy.

He also rejoices over Jolee. Just as she is.

The mark of a zebra, when the problem won't be fixed or the circumstance doesn't change, is to do what is unnatural. *Let it be.* Accept the situation as what God deems necessary and good for you becoming like Jesus, as Paul requesting relief from his thorn (2 Corinthians 12:8). He did not remain unfit, anxious, or gloomy about the future. Instead, he let the Son break through the storm by finding contentment in his weaknesses and embracing them.

For the sake of Christ, then, I am content with weaknesses, insults, hardships, persecutions, and calamities. For when I am weak, then I am strong.

2 Corinthians 12:10 ESV

Sometimes we accept the reality of brokenness that yet has no solution, sickness without cure, and pain where there is no relief as necessary. God still heals. He raises the dead and calls those who are not as though they are. He is able. But He is not obligated to my will and whim when I want my definition of wholeness.

When you and I accept the unacceptable, allowing the Son to break through the storm, we will look different.

God is our refuge and strength,

an ever-present help in trouble.

Therefore we will not fear, though the earth give way

and the mountains fall into the heart of the sea,

though its waters roar and foam

and the mountains quake with their surging

Psalm 46:1-3 NIV

BECOMING VISIBLE—

I know the difficulty required to let your situation be. I've felt the urge to run to my familiar wallpaper rather than pray for God to use my inabilities in the middle of the pack. Make Paul's pronouncement your own today. Pray it until you can live it. Fail in it forward, my friend:

For the sake of Christ, then, I am content with _____

_____. *For when I am weak, then I am strong.*

DAY 36:
FAILING FORWARD FEAT #4

The fight for joy in Christ is not a fight to soften the
cushion of Western comforts. It is a fight for strength to live
a life of self-sacrificing love.

~John Piper [61]

We have talked a lot about joy in the last few days. Make no mistake, your joy will require a fight. The purpose of this failing forward adventure is to prepare you for how to fight for joy not once, not twice, but regularly.

To date, we have learned that God is the giver of joy.

*May the God of hope fill you with all joy and peace as you
trust in him, so that you may overflow with hope by the
power of the Holy Spirit.*

Romans 15:13 NIV

David models what you and I can do in our fight for joy in Psalm 43, providing us a perfect example to follow. Use it as a resource for making forward progress in becoming more like Jesus. Read Psalm 43:1-5.

Call on God for Help

The first action David takes is to call on the Lord to defend him against his enemies (43:1). This we have already learned to do, but it's a glorious reminder of where we need to start.

Practice pouring in assurances of Who God is and why He is reliable. Read Psalm 16:11 below. Also check out Numbers 23:19, Psalm 68:19-20, and Psalm 84:11-12.

You make known to me the path of life; in your presence there is fullness of joy; at your right hand are pleasures forevermore.

Psalm 16:11 ESV

In verse two, juxtaposed with his declaration of God being his refuge, David openly and honestly questions God's distance from him. He feels rejected by God because his circumstances remain bleak.

... Why do I go about mourning because of the oppression of the enemy?

Psalm 43:2 ESV

Soon David finds himself in such a mental and spiritual crisis he recognizes it is time to turn this boat around. He simply moves his eyes off his problems and onto his God.

Send out your light and your truth; let them lead me; let them bring me to your holy hill and to your dwelling!

Psalm 43:3 ESV

Move Your Eyes Off Your Problems and Onto God

David knows from experience that if he will stop looking at the situation and focus on the One who is faithful to him, he will move out of his depressive funk. You and I can do the same thing.

Focus on Scripture

The next right move is to turn to truth. Focus on verses that speak of God's faithfulness, like Psalm 92:4 below, and 2 Timothy 2:13, 1 Thessalonians 5:23-24, and 2 Thessalonians 3:3. Get these running through your mind and heart rather than what you are lacking in your situation.

For you make me glad by your deeds, LORD; I sing for joy at what your hands have done.

Psalm 92:4 NIV

Hold on by Praise and Worship

David is a real person. Struggling. But the struggle and the unknowns will not keep him from preaching to himself in his present badness to hold on to hope.

Your praise and worship amid whatever you are going through can be a game-changer. For certain, it can be a joy-sustainer. As you are slinging mud in your fight for joy, do not forget the significance praise brings.

CHAPTER 5

UNCOVERING THE YOU GOD DESIRES

Becoming the zebra—making change a reality in my life—all sounds well and good. But how do I actually make it happen? Is that what you were thinking?

There is nothing magical or unattainable about it. Let's go further, seeking out the tools and skills needed to uncover the person God desires and enables you to be right where you are, in your personality and shortcomings. You need to know there is nothing to stop you from being fully equipped for adopting the striking visibility that is Christianity lived out in normal everyday life. Sometimes it helps to have a friend leading the way.

DAY 37:
CHANGE YOUR LENS

"You could be a winner!"

It's happened to you. The envelope arrives in your mailbox from the Publisher's Clearing House Sweepstakes announcing you as the winner! The graphic is so lifelike and believable, you might as well enter and let those checks roll in. Maybe you send your entry back. I ponder the winning possibility until I reach the porch, where reality hits. By the time I have crossed the kitchen, I remember the odds: a gazillion to one (or 2.4 billion to one in all accuracy[62]). I will not be a winner. Not today, and probably not ever. My entry lands in the garbage.

Odds for me winning the Sweepstakes were about the same as missing a headlong collision with badness in my life. Throw on the requirement of joy to become perfect and complete? Yep. That sounded like the irrational God of my childhood. What didn't jibe with me in my reluctant negativity was the verse that follows:

If any of you lacks wisdom, let him ask God, who gives generously to all without reproach, and it will be given him.

James 1:5 ESV

Surely James couldn't mean *me*. This was probably one of those "you could be a winner" schemes. Surely *any* and *all* were reserved for the *some* and a *few*. My brain naturally ran everything through the wallflower filter. But becoming the zebra taught me to see differently, using a single strategy: Stop. Look. And study.

Stop with the words that naturally cause you to pause when reading Scripture. In this verse, from my perspective, absolutes like *any*, *all*, and *without* are problematic. Stopping invites me to look more closely at the context, read it again, and consider the surrounding verses.

At this point, I investigate further, *looking* into the context surrounding the verse in question. I might check it out on bible.com in another translation to see if that makes a difference. If I am not satisfied all means all, or if I fear I might be misreading it through my cloudy vision, I take my investigation one last step.

My laptop becomes a mechanism to *study* the text. BibleHub.com is my favorite free electronic resource, but there are plenty of options including blueletterbible.com, biblegateway.com, and biblestudytools.com. At other times, a physical study Bible is helpful. Today, we are not poor on study tools at our fingertips. Taking advantage of what we have is the real struggle, so seize the moment. Make study a habit. Maybe bookmarking these sites is your first step.

In this verse, my wallflower lens was steering me wrong once again. I am a bona fide winner. And the chance of you being one, too, is a whopping 100%. How can I be sure? This God who gives wisdom to any who ask and who gives generously to all is literally the *Giving God*. He's not simply a God who enjoys giving, or a God gifted in giving. James does not present to us the God who gives. Giving is the very essence of who God is. He is the Giving God.[63]

If you then, who are evil, know how to give good gifts to your children, how much more will your Father who is in heaven give good things to those who ask him!

Matthew 7:11 ESV

BECOMING VISIBLE—

When reading a verse you question or don't fully understand, be sure to use the zebra strategy. Stop. Look. And study. Take a minute to investigate the resources suggested today and select one to try the next time you need to study something you don't understand.

DAY 38:
YOUR NEED FOR WISDOM

If any of you lacks wisdom, let him ask God, who gives
generously to all without reproach, and it will be given him.

James 1:5 ESV

As I mentioned before, it took only hours to recognize there was more going on with our little girl now ours than the medical issue surrounding her heart defect. Daily life illuminated holes with weird deficiencies, leaving more questions about how best to love and instruct her. Identifying the root of the problem turned out to be a challenge. After four years, across different cities filled with doctor's appointments, therapies, genetic testing, and evaluations, we located an entity in one of the top medical centers in the country that specializes in international adoption. We praised God eagerly, making the appointments, providing our insurance information, and setting our hopes of finally getting some answers.

The long-anticipated day arrived, filled with more evaluations and interviews. Then my bubble of hope burst. Even after I spelled out for the specialist what we thought might be going on with our daughter, she had no ideas. She had no diagnoses, no tests, no treatments. The expert offered zero expertise. And that was that. A long road to nowhere. The end of what help existed.

With our resources spent and hope depleted, we drove home empty. Tears streamed down my face for hours. Five college degrees between my husband and myself combined with four years of trying everything known to man on the subject, and still no answers. Our only hope was divine intervention. The one thing we could do was ask God to teach us what we needed to know in order to do what He had called us to do. So, we prayed our empty, answerless guts out. Actually, we begged. More than money, education, a listening ear, or patience to endure, we needed wisdom. Wisdom for navigating life day to day, situation by situation. Without it, we were on the fast track to ruining our family.

It's this kind of neediness with which God can work. It's not that we failed to petition Him previously on the subject. Heaven knows we had. If there is only one lesson learned doing life with Jo, it's the truth of James 1:5. I do not know what is best. But I know God will provide the answers I need to get to the next moment, the following step, or tomorrow's meeting on her behalf.

My only hope lies in the promise that God will give me the wisdom for which I ask, and He will give it without beating me up about how many ways I've messed the whole thing up along the way. There is no condemnation for you and your conundrums either, my friend. So you tried to solve the problem on your own, and it all went south. Don't fear receiving an "I told you so," from the Father. He's not like us. God is not waiting to jab us with a "teachable moment" when we can hardly suck back enough air for the present moment. Browbeating is not His style.

Just come. You don't know what to do? Don't have anyone to ask? Perfect. Let God be your teacher. I know He is equal to the task (Psalm 119:99), delighting in giving you the wisdom you need.

Open wide your mouth and I will fill it.

Psalm 81:10 NIV

BECOMING VISIBLE—

What do you want God to fill your mouth with today? In what ways do you need wisdom in this season?

Day 39:
Come in Closer

Draw near to God, and he will draw near to you.

James 4:8 ESV

When I purchase tickets for a live performance, like a Broadway musical or a concert downtown, my kids know to bring binoculars. The seats are sure to be up three flights of stairs, in the top tiered balcony. The cheap seats. Oh, I'd love to sit near the orchestra pit or on the first level ground floor. But the expense would inhibit our going at all. The cost for coming in closer is simply too great.

That's sort of how I was living my life—counting the cost of coming in closer. In the beginning, it was difficult to believe any other seats were for me, but James makes it clear, every child of God is invited to come in closer. So, I gave it a try. You know, like making the commitment to start doing sit-ups every morning. You know you should. It would be good for you, and you will feel better for doing it.

Closer for me meant making time with the Lord the first priority of my day. It required getting out of bed earlier than the baby, the husband, and the toddler, without an alarm. Drawing near called for more time I didn't have. Less sleep. Sleep I needed. And effort. All that personal "I would rather" garbage keeping me in the balcony all those years became my battle. Getting me up without the aid of an alarm seemed an impossible feat in an old creaky house with a baby with bionic ears, but those were the terms. I made a deal with the Lord that if He woke me up, I would get out of bed and seek Him.

What happened from the next morning forward is nothing

short of miraculous. The next morning, and most mornings of the last twenty years, God has been true to His side of the deal. Each morning I would simply wake up before everyone else in the house. It wasn't always at the same time, just earlier than my people arose. Enough time to come in closer. Honestly, most of the time, it still felt like a sit-up's regimen.

That first year, on my birthday, I woke up at 4:30 a.m. Frankly, I was annoyed. My mental response was more of a complaint, "Can't a girl catch a break, Lord? It's my birthday." Almost immediately, before I could even plant my disappointed feet on the ground, I felt an interruption to my rant. The same way I have recognized the Holy Spirit in my life before, nudging me, reminding me of things, or guiding me, I felt a response to my complaining. It was as if the Lord was happy. So excited, He could hardly stand it, saying, "*I know it's your birthday! And I couldn't wait any longer. It's 4:30! Happy Birthday!*" rang out in my head, making a celebratory awakening all the way to those feet, throughout my entire being.

This—from a Negative Nellie preparing for her obligatory holy sit-ups. It's not the sort of thing normally reverberating through the head and heart of Cheri Strange. No. It wasn't *me*. It was *Him*. Drawing near to me. Me? All this time I had been making myself get out of bed, to do the right thing, and try to be the best average Christian girl I could be. Never, not once, did I think God could actually take pleasure in drawing near to *me*. That's just in the Bible for other people.

At least that's what I believed, until that day.

Yet the LORD longs to be gracious to you; therefore he will rise up to show you compassion. For the LORD is a God of justice. Blessed are all who wait for him!

Isaiah 30:18 NIV

BECOMING VISIBLE—

He had to shake me silly to know this reality. I was a tough sell.

Draw near to God and He will draw near to you.

There is an easier way. Try it for yourself. You don't need to leap off the balcony. Just come in closer. What is one move you can make or one step you can take? Remember, the benefits of closer will always exceed the cost.

DAY 40:
BELIEVING TO SEE

But let him ask in faith, with no doubting, for the one who doubts is like a wave of the sea that is driven and tossed by the wind.

James 1:6 ESV

This time, she was ready. The young woman sitting before me shared how her dad promised her something and of his habitual lack of reliability. But this time, when he didn't make good on his promise, she was able to keep her expectations low. It was her high point of the week.

During the awkward extended pause from the other girls in the room, I wondered if she hadn't just nailed a coping mechanism you and I use when it comes to our relationship with God the Father and prayer. Thoughts like, "Why get my hopes up if He's not going to come through for me again?" are likely more common than we would like to admit.

James warns us about this type of negativity, but he calls it rightly, *unbelief,* which is sin (Hebrews 3:12). So how can a Christian get beyond it? How can we possess a faith that overcomes those powerful feelings of doubt?

This is another place the mud-slinging exercise of failing forward with that One Year Bible saved me from myself. It caused me to be in the Psalms more than ever in my life, and that is where I discovered how true to life they proved to be.

David faces this very dilemma in Psalm 27 where he first declares his faith in God, his fearlessness in the face of his enemies because

125

of God, and his personal sense of assurance that God will bring the victory in his situation (Psalm 27:1-6). Then the Psalm takes a slight turn in verse seven, where he asks God to hear his prayer, with a plea not to hide from him. Then he gets a little more desperate in asking him not to turn him away and forsake him. It's like his faith is slipping because by verse twelve, he asks that God not give him up to his enemies. Then in the very next verse, he is back, firmly stating his belief and confidence in a God who can and will come through for him.

I had fainted, unless I had believed to see the goodness of the
LORD in the land of the living.

Psalm 27:13 KJV

David is admitting he is at the end of his ability to trust God. And you can imagine all the good reasons the enemy would offer for why God should forsake him. David is at the end of himself for holding it together. But, shouldn't he have it the other way around? David "believed to see." Isn't seeing believing?

Not if you are David. While he was in the middle of the madness, he gave an all-out effort toward the one thing he thought would get him through: believing God in the dark. David said, *"If I had not believed to see* (what I could not see in the dark) *I would have fainted."* So, he does what you and I must do when we, too, are at our wits' end. *Believe to see.*

Faith shows the reality of what we hope for; it is the evidence
of things we cannot see.

Hebrews 11:1 NLT

BECOMING VISIBLE—

Are you stuck in disappointment like my teenaged friend? If you find you are at the end of yourself, you are in the right place to follow David's example, to believe to see.

Day 41:
Hopeful Expectation

Your faith is the target that all the errors are shot at.

~Charles H. Spurgeon[64]

Belief. Yes, that's the bottom-line issue here. "Let him ask in faith," records James (1:6 ESV), believing God is going to be there, able and eager to meet you in your need, plain and simple. It doesn't have to result from a spirit-filled service or a personal mountaintop moment. You and I just need to ask, petitioning God for help. It seems so simple. We don't need to deserve it. We don't even need to clean up our faces, for He "gives generously to all without reproach" (James 1:5 ESV). Then why do we hold back like we are afraid to let Him come in closer?

Have you ever been to a wedding where they seemed to underestimate the number of guests? The women charged with cutting the cake wield a miracle with their knives, so that what ends up on your plate is paper thin to ensure every guest enjoys a slice. What if we assume God operates similarly, spreading His goodness wide and thin into smaller pieces to have enough for all humanity? That's not how God works, but it is occasionally how we feel, because it's what you and I might do.

How often do we perceive God with limitations on His resources, like we might have stepped in the prayer line one person too late? So, James emboldens us—begs us, almost, to believe and remember with whom we are dealing. The Giving God does not behave like the wedding cake cutter. He's not stingy with His goodness, cutting it into smaller and smaller pieces.

He has removed our sins as far away from us as the east is from the west.

Psalm 103:12 TLB

[His mercies] are new every morning.

Lamentations 3:23 ESV

... the love of Christ ... surpasses knowledge.

Ephesians 3:19 ESV

Oh, the depth of the riches and wisdom and knowledge of God! How unsearchable are his judgments and how inscrutable his ways!

Romans 11:33 ESV

These truths point us away from the line of anticipating disappointment. I've stood there. It will always fail you. But God will not.

Fight to believe. Buckle down in your resolve like the woman Jesus encounters in Matthew 15:21-28. All we know is that she is a Syrophoenician and believes Jesus can help her. Jesus offers her a, "Sorry, sweetheart, I just ran out of cake," sort of answer. "It isn't right to take the children's bread and throw it to the dogs" (Matthew 15:26 CSB). It sounds brutish, but scholars believe it was to amplify her belief, because she does not relent.[65]

Maybe it was her need, or the reality of miracles witnessed. Perhaps she listened to the words of Jesus and believed He was who He claimed to be. Whatever the motivation, her response was brilliant.

"Yes, Lord, yet even the dogs eat the crumbs that fall from their masters' table."

Matthew 15:27 ESV

The woman didn't ask for a place at the table. She was fine being an unnamed fixture in the room, convinced Jesus could help her in only the way a Savior could. That kind of response—believing, with no doubting—garnered her request.

It's just another tale of insignificance. Someone who arrived at the end of herself with a mountain of problems. Jesus was her only hope.

Write this down: The Giving God doesn't give crumbs.

For the LORD God is a sun and shield; the LORD bestows favor and honor. No good thing does he withhold from those who walk uprightly.

Psalm 84:11 ESV

BECOMING VISIBLE–

Is there something you hesitate to pray about because you are afraid God won't have miracle enough? Don't allow fear of disappointment to keep you from asking for what you need. Make your way past the end of yourself to Jesus and let Him be your only hope. Today. Write out your request, confident God is able and willing. No good thing will he withhold from you.

Day 42:
Cultivating Resilience

Blessed in the man who remains steadfast under trial, for when he has stood the test he will receive the crown of life, which God has promised to those who love him.

James 1:12 ESV

We have a set of long stem crystal glasses nestled in the recesses of the highest kitchen cabinet. The set is fragile, and I don't want to end up with a pile of stems and shards. But our everyday dinnerware is a different beast.

That stuff is dumbfounding. They make these pieces out of some mesmerizing acrylic material that has enabled a decade's worth of daily use and hundreds, if not thousands, of cycles through our dishwasher. Cups have dropped repeatedly. Plates slammed against surfaces. Abuses untold have occurred when Mom's not in the room, to be sure, and not a single piece broken. The set is indestructible.

Experts suggest[66] we are becoming less and less like my tough and tenacious dinnerware and more like the crystal—too fragile to navigate. It seems our culture is lacking in resilience. We don't have what it takes to cowgirl up again and again like in earlier days. The rates of depression, loneliness and suicide have skyrocketed compared to previous decades, and that is without the infusion of a worldwide pandemic. We have turned over the reins for our wellbeing to forces outside ourselves, so we should not be shocked to find this phenomenon occurring in our families or run amuck in our communities and schools.

When James writes about remaining steadfast under trials, he means for us to develop this skill. Here, it's more temptation than general trouble,[67] and the need is to become immovable in the face of temptation—to find some personal grit to meet up with our faith.

Personal grit defines Agnes Wilkes, the widow who insisted on feeding me and my husband every other Sunday for as long as we were in her community. Agnes was eighty-seven at the time and lived alone on her farm. What I remember most was her ability to tolerate heat to the touch. Agnes could reach into a blazing oven and touch whatever was cooking with her bare hands to determine if it was ready. She also preferred washing dishes with blistering hot water. Ms. Agnes casually doused her hands in and out while carrying on a conversation. My hands, in comparison, felt half cooked every time they skimmed the surface. That woman wore decades of personal grit on her sleeves.

I fear sweet Agnes is a dying breed. We as a culture are losing our grit. Fragile. That's what we are. If we are going to stand against temptation, we must cultivate more resilience into our lives. Foster fortitude. Recognize life does not work out as well as it looks on Instagram. Then pour oodles and oodles of this quality into our families and spheres of influence.

A flimsy and frail people tend to shy away from Going and Showing, falling prey to unbelief, discouragement and defeat. What can we do? How can we find the fortitude, take the responsibility, and reject our need for external reinforcements? It's simply one decision or choice at a time, over time.

The fear of man brings a snare, But whoever trusts in and puts his confidence in the LORD will be exalted and safe.

Proverbs 29:25 AMP

BECOMING VISIBLE—

Think about how you currently rely on external motivators and reinforcements (like social media or accolades from friends). What is one thing you can do to move from needing and depending upon these outside forces to only relying on who God declares you to be? Choose one.

DAY 43:
DEVELOPING A SIN-DEFEATING STRATEGY

Everybody's not going to understand where God has called
you to go, but that is not an excuse for you not to go there.
Then, when He puts you in certain places, it's a spiritual
warfare to stay there.

~CeCe Winans [68]

I don't eat chocolate.

Before you slam the book shut and become a hater—know it's not
that I don't love chocolate. I really do. Especially Cadbury, but any
variety will do. After recognizing chocolate as a consistent trigger for
my recurrent migraines, I had to make a choice. It was a turbulent
inner struggle to satisfy my cravings for sweet gooey goodness, or
choose to get through the day with the cognitive wherewithal to put
my shirt on right-side out. This kind of inner conflict is what James
addresses when he calls the reader to remain steadfast under trials.

Blessed is the man who remains steadfast under trial, for
when he has stood the test he will receive the crown of life,
which God has promised to those who love him.

James 1:12 ESV

In this second use of the word "trial," James uses a Greek word
that refers to inner struggles or temptations.[69] It's as if James is
pointing us past the difficulty to the reward. Yes. Temptations will
come. That is our reality, regardless of who you are. In fact, you don't
even need to go looking for them.

Remember Joseph, the hated brother sold to Egypt as a slave? He was forced to work in Potiphar's house (Genesis 39:1), where the boss's wife came to him "day after day" tempting him to sin (Genesis 39:10). He didn't seek her out. Joseph was minding his own business, doing everything right. Still, evil sprang up in relentless pursuit of him.

Peter tells us Satan is roaming around like a lion waiting for someone to devour (1 Peter 5:8). No one gets a pass. And the enemy knows how to tailor make trials for you and your weaknesses in your feeble moments. What's a zebra in training to do?

You and I need a sin-defeating strategy as part of our plan. Genesis tells us about Joseph's strategy. He refused to be in the pursuer's presence (Genesis 39:10). Job understood this method as he expressed his own strategy, "I have made a covenant with my eyes; how then could I gaze at a virgin?" (Job 31:1 ESV).

Think about where you most often experience defeat. How can you fight against giving in? Your tactics might resemble me dropping chocolate out of my diet. I like to eat chocolate. But if my desire for chocolate exceeds my commitment to days without debilitating headaches, then I cannot display bite-sized candy bars in the crystal bowl on my dining room table. I won't buy them, nor can I peruse the candy aisle at the grocery store. My family will not be getting homemade delicacies that tempt me for dessert. Instead, alternatives without chocolate will satisfy my cravings.

I'm simplifying the message for the sake of example. What James is telling us is more consequential than persevering with a chocolate-free diet. If we succeed, James promises the "crown of life." My wallflower reaction is, "Really? Sounds sort of fantastical and unachievable." But my zebra discernment helps me to recognize this crown of life is the promise to experience "life in its completeness."[70] Life in its wholeness and entirety, accessible to you and me. Life, also available to any believer who will take seriously the call to remain steadfast.

I have stored up your word in my heart, that I might not sin against you.

Psalm 119:11

No temptation has overtaken you that is not common to man. God is faithful, and he will not let you be tempted beyond your ability, but with the temptation he will also provide the way of escape, that you may be able to endure it.

1 Corinthians 10:13 ESV

BECOMING VISIBLE–

Based on today's readings, what is one strategy you can begin incorporating into your life? What, my friend, needs to be in your sin-defeating strategy? Seek hard after the "crown of life." It's superior to anything we think we want.

Day 44:
Wisdom Beyond You

Knowledge comes, but wisdom lingers.

~Alfred Lord Tennyson[71]

If you are still wondering how a wallflower like me finds herself in the front, rest assured, I came kicking and screaming. The stage is not my comfort zone, and leading is not my place in line, but God finds it necessary and good for me to be in both spaces. If my life were up to me, I would be somewhere in obscurity. Most likely, you would find me teaching a handful of high school students history or economics. My natural hang-out zone is the back corner, holding up the wall. So put away any notions of my successful navigation through these life lessons and exercises because I crave the spotlight.

I write, stand, and post about what I would rather keep private because this journey has been effective. I can do what is beyond me—completely outside of my personality, because I know it is obedience for me.

For many years, I complained of inadequacies and misidentified callings. Today, I understand it all as sort of a hedge of protection. Look at James, the prophet Jeremiah, and certainly Moses. None were looking for fame, recognition, or to be in the front when the call came for them to leave their comfortable corners. What it did was force each one to cultivate a reliance on One greater than themselves. No matter who you are or from what generation, someone from the middle school locker room always beckons you back.

That's where you will find me, again, as a different drama unfolds. I volunteered with a Christian organization, and they eventually asked me to take up a specific leadership role in the front. It was a large responsibility, so they requested I gather a team of women to help lighten the load and share the vision. I accepted and began prayerfully asking individuals to serve with me. Unbeknownst to me, another woman craved my spotlight. She was building up her own reputation as The Leader, swaying my recruits. It's not that I mind passing the baton, but this one wasn't mine to hand over. Did I mention this was voluntary?

This sort of yada-yada garbage happens in churches, HOA's, the Girl Scouts, and every junior high in America. It's where factions enter, bitterness grows, and contempt erupts. Nothing good comes from it, but take note. You and I can be guilty of instigating this drama as well as being on the receiving end. There is a real need for you and I to seek wisdom beyond ourselves.

Somehow, we always find a way back to the middle school locker room whether we want to be there or not. How we act when we get dragged back to the stench makes all the difference. James offers wise advice.

Who is wise and understanding among you? By his good conduct let him show his works in the meekness of wisdom. But if you have bitter jealousy and selfish ambition in your hearts, do not boast and be false to the truth. This is not the wisdom that comes down from above, but is earthly, unspiritual, demonic. For where jealousy and selfish ambition exist, there will be disorder and every vile practice. But the wisdom from above is first pure, then peaceable, gentle, open to reason, full of mercy and good fruits, impartial and sincere.

James 3:13-17 ESV

Christians sometimes behave badly. We cloak our words and actions in truth when it's actually personal pride. That's the message here: guardrails for our hearts, to be careful about our motives. If we are looking to stand out and be seen or heard because of our own ambition, nothing good will come from it. We cannot lose sight of John the Baptist, who so aptly declared, "He must increase, but I must decrease" (John 3:30 ESV).

If you finished that previous paragraph throwing up your hands, feeling completely inadequate, knowing you don't measure up, you are so right. Do not attempt navigating your smelly locker room dramas on your own. You don't have what it takes. Neither do I.

I lift up my eyes to the hills.
From where does my help come?
My help comes from the LORD,
who made heaven and earth.

He will not let your foot be moved;
he who keeps you will not slumber.

Psalm 121:1-3 NIV, 1984

BECOMING VISIBLE—

Before you act first and ask for wisdom later, consider today's truth. Take stock of your own motivation before you make a power move, begin increasing your leverage on social media, or feel like becoming a person of influence. Get a sober sense of your need. A good practice here is to hesitate before you retaliate; or pause before you pounce no matter if you find yourself on the offensive or defensive side. Ask yourself, does my response reflect wisdom that is pure, peaceable, gentle, open to reason, full of mercy and good fruits, impartial and sincere? If not, ask for it. Fail forward.

Day 45:
Good Exceptionalism

Don't settle for a normal life. Not when you can enjoy the wonderful weirdness of being who God created you to be.

~Craig Groeschel[72]

I wish I were funnier. Don't get me wrong, I love to laugh. I need to laugh. If you haven't guessed, I'm not the life of the party. My personality overflows with drive and focus—telling jokes seems to come off awkward to the listener. So radically apparent is my lack, I pray for humor graces. But when I am honest, my double dose of serious has been one of the most effective strategies the enemy uses for keeping me in the shadows.

You may not struggle with a scarcity of hilarity, like myself, but we are not so different. Most of us with straight hair would love curls. Those who cannot tan wish they could. The short would rather be tall. Those with timid, introspective personalities long to be more outgoing, while the gals who are yearn for anonymity. We are all convinced our lives are better fitted with what we don't possess.

Sometimes you and I try to discern God's will for our lives. We search it out, even step into that calling. Scared. Unprepared. And it's been a flop. We quickly discover how powerless and inept we are at whatever we thought we were to do. As we visualize how things could be better, the common denominator is us. If you were different, and if I were, too, everything would change.

What if it is me that's all wrong? What if I'm just too serious, making melancholy mountains out of every molehill? Too unapproachable and scary to be the ministry leader or friend or parent these roles require?

Ahh. There it is.

That's the deception.

Do not be deceived, my beloved brothers. Every good gift and
every perfect gift is from above …

James 1:16-17 ESV

Familiar with all of your weaknesses and failings, God has given you the magnificent gift of uniqueness. That is the framework for viewing God's vision of you. For what He is asking you to do, where, and when, no one else is better fitted. There will be some who can only relate to the Gospel from someone with your experience, possessing your personality, hearing it your way. To believe anything less is deception at its finest.

Jesus needed to capture the attention of the world within three years. Yet there was nothing about Him that would cause us to take notice (Isaiah 53:2). He was so ordinary in appearance that more than once, He slipped through crowds away from the religious authorities (Luke 4:30; John 10:39). On the night of his arrest, Judas identified Jesus by a kiss, which means, even after all the miracles and ministry, He wasn't distinct (Mark 14:44).

Did this factor limit His life's mission? No. He boldly issued hard truths without sinning (John 14:6), and turned over tables in His perfect right (Matthew 21:12). Jesus exhibits the qualities and strengths necessary for the situations into which God sent Him, "for the gifts and the calling of God are irrevocable" (Romans 11:29 ESV).

I wish I were funnier. But the reality that I'm not a humorist does not negate my calling to serve God with my life. Trust God with your exceptionalism.

I cry out to God Most High, to God who fulfills his purpose
for me.

Psalm 57:2 ESV

BECOMING VISIBLE—

It's a great time to change your triggers and take your promises back. Let's at least close the doors of deception. Hide or unfollow every account on your social media platforms that triggers you negatively (by comparison, causing you to feel less than) or leads you to doubt who God is calling you to be. Replace these with encouragement or what speaks life, worth, and truth to you.

Day 46:
Failing Forward Feat #5

Know this, my beloved brothers: let every person be quick to hear.

James 1:19 ESV

You might enjoy the mountains, but the Stranges are beach people. On one occasion, when Chad and I escaped alone on a get-away, we splurged for a guided tour, snorkeling off the reef in the Caribbean.

The day began on a boat shared with a different group embarking on a scuba diving adventure. As we neared the reef, our guide dropped off the divers and moved us to another location. He gave us some instructions about the pickup and simply motioned us to jump off the boat. After a moment's hesitation, my husband jumped off the side into the ocean. I followed suit. Immediately, the boat left us to return to the scuba diving location, as promised.

That's when my husband freaked. He missed the part about dropping us off and then returning to pick us up. Chad understood "get off the boat now," by watching the hand-motions to disembark the boat. He then made an assumption. Not understanding the actual instructions led him straight into panic.

Lickety split, he forgot all about the wonders of creation below in favor of worrying how to get us the two miles back to shore before the sun went down. What we expected to be a fun adventure escalated into a life-threatening situation. His protective nature overrode any chance of a boat full of strangers returning in time, so we started swimming toward land.

Half an hour later, the guide located his "strays." He helped us re-board the boat, but not without chastising us for leaving the area using a few choice Spanish words, wanting to know why we didn't listen.

James understands we can get it all wrong. You and I often listen like Chad and I that day with the tour guide. Maybe your situation is too chaotic and one more element won't stick. God's Word just falls to the ground. Or maybe you can hear, but it sounds like a foreign language. Like Chad, instead of asking, you make assumptions. Sometimes we get it right. Other times we swim for our lives, misinformed.

Did you know that one of the greatest strengths of a zebra is her ability to hear well?[73] It's a defense mechanism alerting her to dangers in time to escape. Her hearing lets her know what she needs to know so she can act. Our vitality depends on our ability to hear well. It's time to rid ourselves of distractions. Put the phone down. Turn off the mental replays of old conversations, real and imagined. Stop thinking about what you will say or do next. Instead, you and I need to *get comfortable with silence and listen*. Listen intently.

Listening well amid a house overflowing with people can be a struggle. I have discovered three strategies.

Pick a version of the Bible on your phone with audio, like www.bible.com, and start listening. Select a reading plan that takes you through the entire Bible. Listen while getting ready in the morning. Or play it while you work in the kitchen or on your daily commute. Give it ten to fifteen minutes per day.

Another opportunity is to redeem the times of your comings and goings by ***listening to a Bible-teaching podcast***. We offer one at www.sheyearns.com/podcasts, called *The Stirring Faith Podcast*, or you can locate one of your choice.

Finally, ***go to church***. Go every week. Lean in, spiritually, to the message from your pastor. God charges that person to shepherd you. Focus on becoming a better hearer, and you will hear better.

Your task is to choose two to incorporate into your week. Write them down and tell a friend. Commit to listening well through your chosen mechanisms for the next thirty days.

PART III
CHAPTER 6

MAKING ROOM FOR VITAL

L iving in a family of ten brings with it a lot of boxes, bins, and loads of too much of I don't know what. The last time we moved, a hurricane hit within the first two months, delaying our unpacking of all that stuff for the next year, which turned into the next. And the next. It's time to let some things go, maybe wave a flag with the garage door wide open announcing, "Come and take it! Really. Please."

The woman wanting to become visible must take measures to let some things go in her life, making room for what is vital in her heart. The commonalities threading these days together are elements you and I need to throw out. It's time to stop storing them in the garage, or closet, or the attic and make a new plan. There is no shame here, my friend—just a raw understanding that purging the rocks and weeds in the soil must take place for the harvest to be bountiful.

Day 47:
Passing Up Impossible

"I can't hear you!"

This fear permeates when I feel I'm missing the target or I've taken a wrong spiritual turn. I think I can hear the Lord and discern His voice in my life. Before stepping out, I read His Word and wait for His leadership. But sometimes when I do, it seems nothing flourishes. I fail at virtually everything I attempt in His Name.

God's hand appears to be guiding and directing other people inside my circle and beyond. I seem to be alone in my defeat. *If His presence is evident everywhere else, why is it not in my life?* I wonder.

When these thoughts cover the landscape of my reality, they obstruct any notion that I can distinguish God's voice from my own. Instead, all I see are the times I have stepped out in daunting or risky endeavors only to be rejected. And there I sit, fruitless. Me. A person charged with leading others to become, well . . . more fruitful. Before I know it, I conclude I can't. I must have heard wrong.

It's taken more years than I would like to admit to navigate how to dismantle this negative thinking; to keep the forward momentum toward becoming my most vibrant and invincible self. But in those years, I have developed a few skills for glimpsing impossible possibilities when I think God's gone on the QT.

Remember, you are not alone in feeling out of step with God's voice. Abraham banked his future on promises it looked like God was breaking. He asked God how his vast inheritance could become a reality when he had no heir (not to mention he was almost one hundred and his wife was decades post menopause) (Genesis 15:2-3).

146

Continue the conversation. When it wasn't working out like Abraham thought it should, he didn't walk away. Even if you don't feel you hear today, cry out to God anyway. When it looks bleak, bear your heart to the Lord in your disappointment, express your lack of understanding, and communicate your concerns, whether or not you feel heard. God will respond. Expect it.

Look to God's Word for His response. God's primary method for speaking into our lives today is through His Word, illuminated by the Holy Spirit. But we can't recognize it if we are not reading it. So, look for God's response. Wait for it. This is what Abraham shows us next.

And behold, the word of the LORD came to him: "This man shall not be your heir; your very own son shall be your heir."

Genesis 15:4 ESV

God gives Abraham an understanding to glimpse the impossible He planned to make possible in his life, and it is enough for him to believe (Genesis 15:6).

What God did for Abraham, He will do for you, in a way you can understand, at the time you need it. Sometimes it will be through a resource or a person. It might be an opportunity, a timely word spoken to you, or possibly a closed door. Even a testimony of one who has gone before you can work miracles. Whatever method He chooses, it will be sufficient to move you forward, believing yes, you can hear Him.

Let me experience your faithful love in the morning, for I trust in you. Reveal to me the way I should go because I appeal to you.

Psalm 143:8 CSB

BECOMING VISIBLE—

Amid the cacophony of voices bidding you to quit, pronouncing your insufficiency, screaming you aren't enough—God says something different. Take these three actions. He is calling you into a divine experience. So march on, sweet sister.

Day 48:
Change Those Old Jeans

For the anger of man does not produce the righteousness of God. Therefore put away all filthiness and rampant wickedness . . .

James 1:20-21 ESV

Our first adoption transpired before there were seminars, books, and workshops available for those in the trenches. Instead, we learned by trial and error. Heavy on the error. Even with all the doctor's appointments, social workers, all those college degrees, and parental experience, there was so much we didn't know, like how to console the inconsolable.

Chloe came to us as a baby. A baby who screamed incessantly. (That's not an exaggeration.) A few months of screaming and a set of ear tubes later, we all had some relief. Still, her dissatisfaction with any situation ran deep, drawing out so much angry wailing she could morph into a sweaty, disheveled wreck beyond my ability to soothe. Most of the time, by the end of the day, we were an unkempt pair.

Any time we ventured out it was the same. A walk in the neighborhood? Head-splitting wailing ensued. The ten-minute drive to church promised a red-hot fit. A simple trip for a treat generated such a temper tantrum, she needed a bath when we returned home. Chloe, by definition, was a hot mess. The activity did not matter. She was like Sam-I-Am about everything, including green eggs and ham. My daughter was not happy in a seat or buggy or swing. She refused all food beyond peas in rice. And getting her to sleep at night could include four hours of unrelenting, ear-piercing screeching, heard across the street.

I'd like to say we had a revelation where a solution surfaced, leading us down the road to recovery and peaceful days. It did not. We simply pushed through the pain for her good and ours, helping her find her fit into the family, and not the other way around. In time, Chloe expanded her security beyond the issues the way you might outgrow a pair of old jeans.

Chloe's transformation reminds me of what you and I do with Truth. Sometimes, on particular points, we don't want to hear what the Bible says. In fact, it can be offensive, sound small-minded, and go against everything that lives inside us. Anger is the result. Maybe we don't even know why, but something about the truths at hand ignites a fire within, possibly even making our blood boil. Okay, so we don't throw a tantrum in the middle of Wal-Mart, but the negative emotions run so high they pull us away from any affection we once held for God and His Word.

James warns us against allowing our anger to flourish (James 1:20). In fact, his language is beyond that of getting angry. Left unchecked, anger leads the person into "filthiness and rampant wickedness" (James 1:21 ESV). This type of behavior will not lead you to becoming the person you long to be, but the sweaty, disheveled mess like my baby daughter. Instead, we can take off this emotional response and the negative heaviness deep within like we would take off a set of clothing. Doing so enables us to receive what is best for us, just like Chad and I have experienced with Chloe.

Are you going to like it? Probably not. Will it be popular? Doubtful. But can you get to perfect and complete without it? Not a chance. We are not created to fit God and the Bible into our existence, but the other way around.

All Scripture is God-breathed [given by divine inspiration] and is profitable for instruction, for conviction [of sin], for correction [of error and restoration to obedience], for training in righteousness [learning to live in conformity to God's will, both publicly and privately—behaving honorably with personal integrity and moral courage];

2 Timothy 3:16 AMP

BECOMING VISIBLE—

If you want to become the confident, vibrant, stand out version of yourself, this anger for wanting everything to fit neatly into your way of seeing needs to go like an old pair of jeans. In other words, you and I can't be a hot mess when it comes to facing off against what we like and don't like about the Bible. Today, begin asking God to reveal these areas to you, restore your hope, and help you receive His Truth.

Day 49:
Playing the Victim

Most people want to make you responsible for the way they
feel. The victim look ain't a pretty one, baby.

~Rachel Wolchin [74]

He said he was going to starve to death, and it was all my fault.
Sounds pretty harsh, doesn't it? I run a tight ship at the Strange
house, but this dire situation involved a piece of paper, a horn, and
my refusal to sign said paper. The paper assured the teacher he prac-
ticed the horn. I knew otherwise. Apparently, the only time he had
to squeeze practicing into his busy pre-teen schedule was mealtime.
You can follow the logic for how his starvation was now my fault. A
tantrum and some tears commenced when I did not sign the paper
or accept the accusation of parental neglect.

We call this recurrent scenario at the Strange house *Playing the
Victim*. It surfaces when a person believes they are not in control of
their own destiny. Life is happening to them. The problem is not
theirs, personally, and they blame someone else. It's your fault, the
girl over there, the teacher, or anyone other than them. If you haven't
taken part, you have likely seen the theatrics in motion.

Playing the Victim differs from being a victim. A genuine victim
is a person who is injured, hurt, or whose rights are violated, who
did not choose it, welcome it, or even see it coming.[75] Playing the
Victim, on the other hand, is a shift in mindset you and I need to
reject. Instead of leading individuals toward resilience and a strong
sense of who they are, Playing the Victim relegates control to external
sources. It's when I blame others to excuse myself.

There was a similar victim game going on in the early Christian church, but the scapegoat was God. Jewish rabbis begged the question of where evil began. They argued if God was the creator of all things, He must be the creator of evil. Therefore, if anything or anyone is to blame for the problem of sin and the evil tendencies of man, it had to be God. So, like my starving son's reasoning, man became a victim of God's actions.[76]

Jesus brings clarity to what man distorted by pointing people to the core issue. Rather than blaming their badness on God or outside influences, He illuminates the personal responsibility for man's sin at the heart level—including sexual immorality, theft, murder, adultery, coveting, general wickedness, deceit, sensuality, envy, slander, murder, pride, and plain foolishness (Mark 7:20-23). When James puts his pen to the subject, he aligns with the teaching of Jesus.

Let no one say when he is tempted, "I am being tempted by God," for God cannot be tempted with evil, and he himself tempts no one. But each person is tempted when he is lured and enticed by his own desire. Then desire when it has conceived gives birth to sin, and sin when it is fully grown brings forth death.

James 1:13-15 ESV

James is not pointing fingers, but showing us the way to freedom. Freedom from our own prison of denial, blame, and continued sin. So, what's a girl to do? How do we move away from this mindset?

Instead of shirking our mistakes as someone else's responsibility, blaming other people for the problem of us, the call is simply to own them. Own your own weaknesses.

Do not let sin control the way you live; do not give in to sinful desires. Do not let any part of your body become an instrument of evil to serve sin. Instead, give yourselves completely to God, for you were dead, but now you have new

153

life. So use your whole body as an instrument to do what is right for the glory of God. Sin is no longer your master, for you no longer live under the requirements of the law. Instead, you live under the freedom of God's grace.

Romans 6:12-14 NLT

BECOMING VISIBLE–

If you lean toward these tendencies, ask God how you can actively fight against giving into the desire to rid yourself of the blame. Rehearse difficult phrases like "It was my fault," and "I did it," and when they're true—use them. When you find yourself unwillingly in the game, graciously help others know you will not be assisting them in kicking the responsibility can down the road.

Day 50:
Dangers in Your Midst

Let us not be surprised when we have to face difficulties.
When the wind blows hard on a tree, the roots stretch
and grow the stronger. Let it be so with us. Let us not be
weaklings, yielding to every wind that blows, but strong in
spirit to resist.

~Amy Carmichael[77]

A move to the big city brought a transition from soccer to lacrosse for my twin boys. All you need for soccer is a pair of shoes, shin guards, and a water bottle. Not so with lacrosse. We showed up to play in the same shoes and water bottles, while the other players donned knee pads, elbow pads, body armor, long metal sticks, and helmets the size of New Jersey. The coach took one look at my boys and announced, "You can't play like that. Someone's going to die."

I'm glad we listened. Even armed in all that garb, the game is a bruiser. A week later, we arrived equipped and ready to rumble.

Too often, you and I show up to whatever is happening in our lives the same way the Strange boys arrived at their initial lacrosse workout. Unprepared. Armed with nothing more than a water bottle. Maybe we didn't know what to expect, or perhaps we failed to plan ahead. The result is the same. Our losses are great and come with long-lasting bruises and damage.

There is a better way to meet the dangers in our midst. We can do something other than get spiritually clocked or retreat to our familiar corners in shame.

Submit yourselves therefore to God. Resist the devil, and he will flee from you.

James 4:7 ESV

James offers a two-step program for dealing with the dangers in our midst: *submit* and *resist*. These work in harmony to defeat what seeks to send us to the sidelines mangled and maimed, so that we can, instead, become striking and vibrantly seen.

Submitting to God involves accepting His plan for salvation. Jesus, as the solitary way to God, is not popular. Being on the right side of socially constructed history, hanging with the majority, does not make something true. Knowing what the Bible says and choosing to believe God over what is popular is your pathway toward victory in the battle to resist whatever comes against you in this arena.

Submitting also involves yielding to God's will for our lives. Often, He doesn't work fast enough. God doesn't fight back like our enemies deserve. The injustice is too much to endure. The silence is too deafening to leave words unsaid. Our plans are better than following His.

My friend, I have the scars and injuries to prove this move is a guaranteed fail. The temptation to leave God in your dust and whack your way to victory is a losing strategy. That's the devil in your ear, sweet girl. It promises sure defeat. Submitting to God's way and will is a fast track toward our victory march.

Another way I have often ended up black and blue is trying to play by my rules, rather than by God's. Obedience is a learned skill, like lacrosse, which we must exercise and practice. James gives us a key strategy that is a ringer every time. *Resist*. Don't do it, chew it, eat it, partake in it, shoot it up, play with it, watch it, say it, or steal it. (You get the drift.) But let me write it again for my own eyes. Resist the temptation to hijack God's good plan and timetable for your own because you believe yours is better. No. Obedience is the path to victory. This move is not as complicated as we make it out to be. Resisting is our winning strategy, well worth the effort. Resist the enemy, in every shape and form, for he must leave you.

We know that our old sinful selves were crucified with Christ so that sin might lose its power in our lives. We are no longer slaves to sin. For when we died with Christ we were set free from the power of sin.

Romans 6:6-7 NLT

BECOMING VISIBLE–

How well are you submitting in the areas of salvation, obedience, and yielding to God's will for your life? Which area needs the most focus and attention? Are you quick to obey? Maybe you are like me and slow to yield your way to His? Star that one on the page giving you the most difficulty. What will you do today in that area that will help ensure you will experience more victory in the future?

Day 51:
Non-Toxic Reflections

It is not my ability, but my response to God's ability, that counts.

~Corrie Ten Boom[78]

Do you know what it's like to feel poor? I say "feel" because by most of the world's standards, the majority in America are wealthy, no matter your standard of living. But if your roots are from humble beginnings, you probably know what it's like not to have what everyone else had for school, to own a couple of pairs of clothes that fit, or to maybe forgo that opportunity because of the cost to participate. Maybe you worked your way through school, or became independent sooner than later so as not to be a burden. This is my personal history. Your circumstances might be different, but the age-old strategies work from the enemy to communicate, *You're not good enough*.

Those words are whispered into your thoughts, hovering over your financial situation, but they mingle into other areas of your life. Before you know it, not having enough is no longer about possessions but *who you are*.

The natural solution to your financial problem becomes getting more. If you could only have more money, more things, better clothes, a cooler car, the ultimate house in the better neighborhood, then, you *would* be enough. But sometimes, you still fail. Who knew the lies would turn out to be, well, *lies*? There you are, still broken, insufficient, and longing for more and to be more.

This business of toxic reflections has been going on for centuries. At some point, James decides against all the hype, arriving at an arresting perspective.

158

Let the lowly brother boast in his exaltation, and the rich in his humiliation, because like a flower of the grass he will pass away. For the sun rises with its scorching heat and withers the grass; its flower falls, and its beauty perishes. So also will the rich man fade away in the midst of his pursuits.

James 1:9-11 ESV

That doesn't even make any sense. How can the lowly "boast in his exaltation?" Why would James suggest something so oxymoronic? The Bible doesn't tell us, per se, but we can investigate. It's not only that these fellow believers are hard up for cash and possessions in the Roman world. The word James uses is more encompassing, meaning poor, crushed, or oppressed.[79] His message is tender toward the one who feels like she is not enough, reflecting the heart of God.

Something about this concept leaps off the page when we look at Gideon. The tale unfolds with bad guys oppressing God's people and ravaging their supplies. Gideon was just a guy, hiding out in a winepress, when the angel greets him.

"The Lord is with you, mighty warrior."

Judges 6:12 NIV

"Mighty Warrior" is not the self-talk package Gideon was preaching to himself alone hiding in the winepress. We tap into Gideon's personal estimation in his response:

And he said to him, "Please, Lord, how can I save Israel? Behold, my clan is the weakest in Manasseh, and I am the least in my father's house"

Judges 6:15 ESV

Gideon's response to God's declaration sounds like our familiar, *I'm not good enough,* mantra: *"How can I," "the weakest," "I am the least."* Yep. It's the same yada-yada battle you and I experience morning after morning.

James encourages us beyond our own toxic reflections to boast in our exaltation because God is not limited in who He calls by what we possess, nor is He bound by our limitations. We should not be, either.

> *What then shall we say to these things? If God is for us, who can be against us? He who did not spare his own Son but gave him up for us all, how will he not also with him graciously give us all things?*
>
> Romans 8:31-32 ESV

BECOMING VISIBLE—

My friend, change your language to yourself and to the God who is for your good. Look up these three verses and add them to your arsenal to defeat what is keeping you from all God has for you.

2 Timothy 1:7

2 Corinthians 2:14

2 Peter 2:9

DAY 52:
FIRES AND WOES

How great a forest is set ablaze by such a small fire!

James 3:5 ESV

What do pickup trucks, rocks, flat tires, and hammers have in common? Each one is responsible for accidentally setting California ablaze. In 1965, a pickup truck owned by Johnny Cash was found to be responsible for destroying over 500 acres and endangering condors. The Mendocino Complex Fire, the largest fire in the state's history, is believed to have been started by the spark from a hammer. Another fire began from a flat tire. And a man went to prison for hitting a rock with his lawn mower in 2004, causing a fire to race through the neighborhood, destroying many homes.[80] These objects are not designed for setting fires. And the operators of the objects had no intention of doing so. Yet it happened—with severe, devastating and even deadly consequences.

The Bible teaches we can be responsible in the same way with our tongues. Maybe we don't set out to burn down a neighborhood, but you and I have likely started something with our mouths that ended in destruction.

*And the tongue is a fire, a world of unrighteousness. The
tongue is set among our members, staining the whole body,
setting on fire the entire course of life, and set on fire by hell.*

James 3:6 ESV

James is not the only one who emphasizes the mischief our mouths can muster (Proverbs 15:4; Psalms 34:13; Ephesians 4:19), but he takes a Sharpie to the issue, underlining and drawing circles around it for emphasis. Or haven't you noticed? Maybe this is a particular struggle for his audience? Perhaps personal experience energized his campaign? Who knows? What we can ascertain is his laser focus on helping the reader recognize how powerful the tongue is.

Honing in on those moments when we have said what we shouldn't is easy. We recognize these as "a world of unrighteousness." You and I don't need any finger wagging to identify our faults there. But what about those that burn down forests, houses and neighborhoods *unintentionally*? The comment to the friend, the sister, the daughter, or your spouse that they remember and will not let you forget. Spoken flippantly. The moments you wish you could get a do-over to hold back your words that cut deeply and fractured greatly. These are the fires of which James warns us.

Can we fix it? Well, that's just it.

But no human being can tame the tongue. It is a restless evil, full of deadly poison.

James 3:8 ESV

We can't. This is the point James is making. Yet we are responsible for our words (Matthew 12:36), just like the mower who went to jail for accidentally throwing the rock that sparked the forest fire. You and I want to be seen. We don't want to *make a scene*. Learning to control our tongues is a necessary and life-giving move. Only God can do the divine work in our hearts. But He has provided the Bible to lead us in the right direction.

Those who control their tongue will have a long life; opening your mouth can ruin everything.

Proverbs 13:3 NLT

BECOMING VISIBLE—

Ask the Lord to put a guard over your mouth (Proverbs 13:3) and protect you from intentionally and unintentionally hurting others with your words. Look up each verse below and record one action you can take to control your tongue better today than you did yesterday. As we pray, taking the actions as we are able, and trusting God to do what only He can do, we will shine brightly in dark places.

Proverbs 10:19

Ephesians 4:29

Ephesians 5:4

Colossians 4:6

Day 53:
The Snob Within

We should be rigorous in judging ourselves and gracious in
judging others.

~John Wesley[81]

Of all the blessings my years have afforded, one of the greatest is
my family. Coming together from three different ethnicities and
four unique cultural regions around the globe brings the beauty of
God's variety into perspective. The nuances of colors, languages, and
cultural variances disprove the snob within screaming, "I'm better
than you." Experience teaches it's just not true. So often, our pride-
ful personal assessment contradicts how we are to love our neighbor
(Mark 12:31). We know this, but the snob within still rears its ugly
head periodically.

Sometimes the snob within appears for reasons other than the
obvious race, economic status, or levels of education so prevalent
today. Recently, like an elephant in the room, the snob emerged two
rows in front of me during a worship service. The reason for the
exhibition? Breathing.

Two women faithfully attend and serve the people of this church,
and have for decades. Currently, one is experiencing debilitating
health issues. She depends on a walker and oxygen tank, which
makes regular palpitating sounds, helping her breathe. The sanctuary
can accommodate her needs on either end of a row. She generally sits
on the far side, near an exit. This day, worshippers filled the room.
Her regular, unobtrusive section was full. This is where the vexation
began.

164

The ushers seated the twosome toward the back center aisle. All was well until the preacher began his message and the snob within the man across the aisle took notice of the rhythmic hum from the oxygen tank. After turning wildly, demonstrating his disgust, he aimed his body toward her, away from the pastor, staring her down, arms crossed, as to shame her for disturbing his worship experience.

My friend fixed her gaze between the pastor and her notes, unmoved. When the snob ran out of ideas for encouraging her to retreat or stop breathing, he, too, returned to the reason he came, but not without obvious irritation engulfing his demeanor. Giving one last over-exaggerated disapproving nod, the man exited the room before the service ended.

The snob within is a jerk when what is within comes out. It has no place in the life of a believer. But oh, is it a struggle. James tenderly but truthfully addresses the issue, using the most prominent example of his day.

My brothers, show no partiality as you hold the faith in our Lord Jesus Christ, the Lord of glory.

James 2:1 ESV

Favoritism based on externals is inconsistent with faith in the One who came to break down all the barriers we might try to use to justify snobbish behavior.[82] In case we do not make the connection on our own, James harkens us back to the Golden Rule, warning that, "If you really fulfill the royal law according to the Scripture, 'You shall love your neighbor as yourself,' you are doing well. But if you show partiality, you are committing sin and are convicted by the law as transgressors" (James 2:8-9 ESV).

The page becomes personal as you and I often wrongfully hold contempt for people different from us. When we do, our problem is sin. The solution is to seek forgiveness and turn away from that behavior. That snob within is a hindrance to all God intends us to become. She needs to be recognized and shut down in every one of us.

Here there is not Greek or Jew, circumcised and uncircumcised, barbarian, Scythian, slave, free; but Christ is all, and in all.

Colossians 3:11 ESV

BECOMING VISIBLE—

Consider how Colossians 3:11 relates to James 2:1-9. Begin asking the Lord to help you release any attitudes and beliefs you may hold, in terms of favoritism, that are contrary to the Gospel. Holding onto these willfully will never lead us to *perfect and complete.*

DAY 54:
THE DIRTY-DIRT

Grace is sufficient even though we huff and puff with all our might to try and find something or someone that it cannot cover. Grace is enough.

~Brennan Manning[83]

I have been one of The Chosen.

My husband and I were traveling through an international airport on our way home from a conference. I heard the alarm sound, and all I could think was, *please be someone else, please be someone else.* By the time the gentleman in blue and black asked me to step out of the security line, I'd already started sweating. I knew something the very thorough TSA agent did not—but soon would—know. In re-shuffling our belongings to make unpacking easier, guess whose suitcase ended up carrying a plethora of dirty underwear, soon to be in panoramic view for everyone to behold? It's the kind of experience that leaves you feeling red in the face, completely exposed.

This is how I imagine James can affect a person at times.

What causes quarrels and what causes fights among you? Is it not this, that your passions are at war within you? You desire and do not have, so you murder. You covet and cannot obtain, so you fight and quarrel. You do not have, because you do not ask. You ask and do not receive, because you ask wrongly, to spend it on your passions. You adulterous people! Do you not know that friendship with the world is enmity with God? Therefore whoever wishes to be a friend of the world makes himself an enemy of God.

James 4:1-4 ESV

The gall.

Wait. Is James sounding a false alarm? Do believers in Christ experience quarrels and fight with each other? Have we desired what's in her closet, on her wrist, to live in her house, or possess her abilities, to the degree we cut one another down, destroying relationships? This is the scenario James addresses. Then the same individuals pray, asking for what they don't possess but want, expecting God to bless them.

Sadly, these believers have acquired more of a taste for the things of their culture (like clothing, houses, entertainment, possessions, power) than a hunger for the things of God. This dirty laundry mirrors what we might see bulging out of the suitcases of believers down the hall, on our own street, or reflected in our own lifestyles and wish lists.

It would be easier to talk about becoming the most invincible version of ourselves if we skipped the dirty unmentionables. Yet, if we want to be seen for who Jesus is making us to be, introspection is essential.

Are your passions warring within you? Can you identify with the relationship difficulties suggested? Do your desires line up closer with the culture or with Jesus? James is sounding the alarm to rifle through your dirty dirt, not to throw us into humiliation and shame, but to move you and me closer to perfect and complete. How?

But he [God] gives more grace. Therefore it says, "God opposes the proud but gives grace to the humble."

James 4:6 ESV

Is your suitcase bulging with the unsightly, like mine? You, my friend, are not a lost cause. The alarm is for alerting us to our desperate need of what only He can fix. Throw the case open. Spread the dirty laundry out before Him. Receive the grace. He has enough. In fact, *He gives more grace.*

How much more?

Well, how much dirty underwear do you have?

BECOMING VISIBLE—

Think about the ways you might align yourself with the world rather than with Jesus. Pull these pursuits or longing or disappointments out like a load of dirty laundry, exposing and confessing each one. Receive the perfect gift of grace that covers all your needs. And then some.

Day 55:
Judgy Judgment

We can never judge the lives of others, because each person
knows only their own pain and renunciation.

~Paulo Coelho[84]

The new Golden Rule of the twenty-first century seems to find its
roots with James.

*There is only one lawgiver and judge, he who is able to save
and to destroy. But who are you to judge your neighbor?*

James 4:12 ESV

What you do is not my business and what I do is not yours.
Does James condone this mindset? Or is he addressing more than
meets the eyes of our contemporary understanding? Honestly, there
must be more to it, because in one chapter, he encourages us to bring
sinners back from wandering away from the truth (James 5:19-20).
That act, by definition, involves the judgment of your neighbor. This
is one of those times when we need to go beyond reading and study
what we find in the text.

Malice and vindictive slander are what we find—of the variety
we know better than to take part in or allow to originate with us. Yet
somehow, we almost don't recognize these behaviors as wrong until
they happen to us.

Take Katie Davis, for example. Directly after her high school
graduation, she seized an opportunity to teach English at an

orphanage in a small village near a city called Jinja in Uganda, as a temporary experience before starting college. But that all changed when a mud hut down the road collapsed on three orphans. One of the girls needed medical attention, and Davis could not locate any living relatives willing to take the girls home. So, rather than sending them to other overcrowded orphanages, she ended up taking them in herself.

She rented a house with enough space to meet their needs. But now she saw what she did not see before. Within eighteen months, ten more girls, abandoned, abused, or whose parents died of AIDS, moved into the house. In addition, she began a partnership to fund a non-profit organization to help educate over four hundred children in the area. As she explains her reasoning, it wasn't that she had a burning desire for adoption. She simply responded to needs God placed in front of her.

But Katie's actions raised a critical eyebrow. She's too young to adopt according to the law of Uganda. Others criticized her for taking care of so many children (although many of those she took in came from families of the same size). Still others were upset with her efforts in general and minimized the work she accomplished.[85]

Can you relate? I've been on the receiving end of vindictive slander. You likely have as well. More than being a receiver of this garbage, I have dished it out. Without knowing all the facts, before the evidence presented itself. Pure malice and true slander.

This I now know: If we desire to lose ourselves to living a Going and Showing Gospel light for His glory rather than our own—we must rid ourselves of the sinful practice of bad-mouthing. There is no other way.

Your kindness will reward you, but your cruelty will destroy you.

Proverbs 11:17 NLT

BECOMING VISIBLE—

Today, I invite you to pray for victory over what you might not have thought you needed victory over. Ask God to give you the courage to hold your judgmental tongue. Not tell the story. Stop the spread of what we don't yet know for a fact. Then and only then will we begin our walk toward vibrant and visible.

Day 56:
Failing Forward Feat #6

Sight is not faith, and hearing is not faith, neither is feeling faith; but believing when we neither see, hear, nor feel is faith; and everywhere the Bible tells us our salvation is to be by faith. Therefore we must believe before we feel, and often against our feelings, if we would honor God by our faith.

~Hannah Whitall Smith[86]

If my life could be characterized by one grotesque, overarching sin, it would be that of filling buckets with holes. If you missed that sin, it's in there. God calls it choosing broken cisterns over the fountain of living water (Jeremiah 2:13). James points out that his readers "ask and do not receive" (James 4:3 ESV) and gives the reason why. It all boils down to the same issue: Unbelief.

Too often, we do not believe God will come through for us. It's an underlying current that flows through every vein of my existence. The result across my life has been an empty bucket, or what Jeremiah called a broken cistern that can hold no water. I feel like God is holding out on me. He cannot be trusted and does not have my best interests in view. At all. (But that's the empty bucket talking.)

My failing forward adventuring has taught me my need to stop the flow of that unbelieving river and get a new bucket. I don't know if I thought it was a personality quirk or blamed it on my upbringing, but for years, I didn't think anything of my tendency to ask while doubting God's willingness or ability to deliver. All that changed when I came to recognize my unbelief for what it is: Sin.

The writer of Hebrews warns us not to have an unbelieving

heart (Hebrews 3:12). As a believer in God, I was sure he was not talking about me. I believed in God. There. Done. Check. Isn't that all I'm responsible for?

I thought so.

James says otherwise.

You believe that God is one; you do well. Even the demons believe—and shudder!

James 2:19 ESV

There is more to this warning. The Amplified Version, Classic Edition shines a light on it, helping me see what I didn't before.

[Therefore beware], brethren, take care, lest there be in any one of you a wicked, unbelieving heart [which refuses to cleave to, trust in, and rely on Him], leading you to turn away and desert or stand aloof from the living God.

Hebrews 3:12 AMPC

A believing heart is so much more than the mental declaration of believing in God as God. Hebrews deals with holey buckets. How can I cleave to one I don't believe will deliver? Can I truly trust in the One who might disappoint me? Is God reliable when I'm unsure I'm important enough to consider?

Well, I was in trouble, holding onto my holey bucket, because anything short of cleaving to, trusting in, and relying on the Living God is blatant sin. Mine was laid bare all over the page.

How do you move from standing aloof to cleaving? Where does the trust come from? How can a person exchange a broken bucket for one that holds water? We might be able to learn a lesson from the Psalmist and an elephant.

174

"The L'ORD will fulfill his purpose for me; your steadfast love,
O L'ORD, endures forever. Do not forsake the work of your
hands.

Psalm 138:8 ESV

There is an old wives' tale of elephants possessing a sixth sense about bridges. Somehow, they have a sense about their reliability. They cross the ones they trust will hold them and refuse to cross those they do not. In June of 1917, it proved true. A traveling circus needed to cross over the bridge on the Sodus Bay on the south shores of Lake Ontario in New York. All the animals who could walk were taken across, but the elephant wouldn't budge. She refused to move. In fact, the trainers ultimately had to take her on an alternative route. It didn't matter if the monkeys and the horses made the trek successfully. What about her? Would the bridge sustain her weight? She didn't think so. Turns out, she was right. The bridge had trouble for the next three renovations and ninety years.[87]

I tend to be like this cautious beauty. It doesn't matter if God helped you across. What if what I need is too heavy, too much trouble, or beyond the limit warranted? Can I trust what I read to be true for me?

The Psalmist is assuring us, the promises of God will hold. Test Him in these. Does His forgiveness extend to *all* of your failings? Is His mercy enough for even your rotten self? And mine? What if you have been like me, swimming in a river flowing with unbelief and negativity for decades? Can you still get a new bucket? Will He or will He not fulfill His purposes for you? What does your God promise?

He promises that He can, indeed, hold what you have entrusted to Him (2 Timothy 1:12). Go on. Start walking. The bridge will hold steady. Your God will not fail you.

Then David said to his son Solomon, "Be strong and
courageous, and take action; do not fear nor be dismayed, for

175

*the LORD God, my God, is with you. **He will not fail you**
nor abandon you [but will guide you in the construction]
until you have finished all the work for the service of the
house of the LORD.*

1 Chronicles 28:20 AMP

BECOMING VISIBLE–

I needed a visual to help make this truth a reality in my life. For thirteen years, I wore a bracelet with the words "Believe God" engraved on it. When I didn't need it anymore, I put it away. Directions for making your own Believe God bracelet are linked in your plan with an additional link for purchasing one if that's more your speed.

PART IV
CHAPTER 7

HOW TO BECOME VIBRANT

You know that feeling you get when you finally begin to notice a difference due to whatever change you decided to make in your life? Maybe you can run an extra mile or lift a box without getting tired. Perhaps the mirror reflects a slight change in your shape or you refrained from saying what you thought in the heat of the moment. That, my friend, is when change moves from simply visible to becoming vibrant. It's when you are full of life, stable in knowing to Whom you belong. And it's the direction you and I are moving, learning what distinguishes a zebra from the herd. More than the habits and behaviors to suspend, becoming vibrant reflects an understanding of Who we live to make known, because that makes all the difference.

Day 57:
Becoming Vibrant

My biggest fear, even now, is that I will hear Jesus' words
and walk away, content to settle for less than radical
obedience to Him.

~David Platt[88]

To become vibrant requires more than a Ponzi scheme. That's for sure. Charles Ponzi was an Italian immigrant who made a fortune telling people what they wanted to hear. No need to work. There was a shortcut to getting rich. His pitch, promising low risk with high benefits, has been swindling people out of their money for centuries. But Ponzi brought both eloquence and efficiency to the game.

He promised high dividends in short return times and delivered. The short-cut to prosperity seemed to work. Early investors were paid high returns from money traded in by later investors. But in reality, there was no real commodity, just fabricated reports. Finally, the scam unraveled as thousands learned they had been bamboozled. Ponzi's overall racket was so effective, the scheme became named after the man who paid the penalty for his success in jail time.[89]

The enemy is adept in Ponzi schemes, making us believe there is a better, shorter way. He whispers sweet nothings like, "You don't need to do it God's way. ""If He really loved you, He would give you X. "And, "Why wait?" Paramount to our success is remembering that a Ponzi scheme will never get us to *perfect and complete.*

James includes himself in reminding us we are all on a broken road aiming for Christlikeness. "For we all stumble in many ways" (James 3:2 ESV). The path toward perfect and complete is marked by failed attempts mixed with bullseyes. Good days and bad. The zebra among the herd is still human, but the vibrant follower of Jesus is learning not to be swayed by intoxicating verbiage from the enemy. Instead, she embraces the Savior and His Word to her, believing God will use her in her imperfections.

The life of Dwight L. Moody illustrates this beautifully. On paper, Moody was nothing more than a shoe salesman from Chicago. He had no degrees or formal education in theology. The man did not set out to become a minister, he simply gave himself to God to use as He could. The ordinary shoe salesman turned evangelist brought the Gospel to over 100 million people across the globe before modern technology.[90]

How does this happen? How do regular people develop this vibrancy and willingness for God to use them any way He sees fit? With an acute awareness of James 3:2. He was not beyond making paramount mistakes. One way he demonstrated his understanding was by invited other Bible scholars to preach at his church, sitting at their feet as a learner, willing to be corrected.[91]

And then one conversation changed his life. In 1872, he traveled to Britain where he met with Henry Varley, another evangelist. Mr. Varley looked at this average individual and saw a zebra. He said something to Moody he would never forget, and you and I should take to heart:

> "The world has yet to see what God can do with and for and through and in a man who is fully and wholly consecrated to Him."[92]

BECOMING VIBRANT–

The same truth holds true today, my friend. The world has yet to see what God can do *with* and *for* and *through* and *in* a woman who is fully and wholly consecrated to Him. Likely there is oh, so much more God can do with this vibrant version of you. Won't you take your average self to the throne? Hold nothing back and only God knows what He will do through you.

Day 58:
Never Forget

Perhaps, my friend, there is no testimony that you can bear,
which will be so useful, so interesting, and so striking, as
the testimony of what you have yourself seen and handled
of the Word of life. Tell the gospel as you find it in the
Bible, but set it in the frame of your own experience of its
preciousness.

~Charles H. Spurgeon[93]

Grandma Rathbun grew up during the Great Depression. Like many others from her generation, it shaped her habits and behaviors for the following decades. Even upon her death, she had harbored storehouses of staples a family could survive on for more than a year. We were up to our armpits in macaroni and canned goods. She never forgot how the world can leave you in dire need. It tempered her very existence, which turned out to be a good thing. The model and lifestyle gave her children the grounding to survive their own difficulties.

Life experiences leave a mark. When we find ourselves wondering or questioning the point of all this desert wasteland in our midst, we should remember—it's not just for us. It's really about them. Are these struggles, these impossibilities—the half-mud-clad fence you are struggling to cover or the transformation you feel for your life's work and purpose? Not so. Just as Grandma Rathbun's life lessons in simplicity and preparation extended beyond her generation for good, your life story reaches past what you can see or comprehend.

Your testimony—that work God is doing in your life, seen and heard in the flesh—is for *them*. The personal zebra transformation we are pursuing is not the sole and solitary reason for all the mess. It's for your children, your neighbors, your parents, for anyone in your sphere of influence. Your vibrancy is significant beyond yourself. It is this very thing God wanted instilled in the Israelites through that desert journey toward the Promised Land.

And he brought us out from there, that he might bring us in and give us the land that he swore to give to our fathers.

Deuteronomy 6:23 ESV

You might recall, there was a shorter way around the proverbial barn. A two-week journey from the Red Sea to the covenanted ease and comfort. But God could foresee the problems in leading them down the path of easy. Guaranteed war. Sure abandonment (Exodus 13:17-18). The stints of waterless days mixed with years of daily following proved purposeful, even essential to their success.

Where have your desert places been? Those seasons of hurt, pain, or misery, and days you didn't know if you would survive that seemed so pointless? Maybe seem pointless still? Why did it all transpire? What is that place—physical, emotional, or space in time—you are so glad not to be today?

Sweet friend, write this truth on the walls of your puzzled memories. He *brought you out* of all of that awfulness, so He might *bring you in.* This truth I live and breathe. For whatever reason, the path to what He promises you requires extended wanderings and suffering. This reality remains: He brought you out so that he might bring you in. You alone in your heartache helps no one. But your experiences and testimony remembered, told in view of Him, makes you striking to a world that needs you to be vibrant in their midst. Someone needs to know what God has done in your life because their life and future may well depend upon it.

He brought me out into a broad place; he rescued me, because he delighted in me.

Psalm 18:19 ESV

BECOMING VIBRANT–

Can you identify any ways God has shown Himself to be bringing you in after those difficult seasons, or are you still waiting? What do you believe will be an impact to those around you if they knew of God's faithfulness to you in those painful and difficult moments of your life?

Day 59:
Receive the Implant

Wherever the Bible has been consistently applied, it has dramatically changed the civilization and culture of those who have accepted its teaching. No other book has ever so dramatically changed the individual lives and society in general.

~John F. Walvoord[94]

Maybe you don't know if or when you are being brought in? How does a person know? I think it has to do with the ability to "hear" God—the way we sometimes feel we can and other times can't. Then there is an element of purpose mixed with His will for our lives.

John shows us we can learn to hear His voice like a sheep hears the shepherd. "The sheep hear his voice, and he calls his own sheep by name and leads them out. When he has brought out all his own, he goes before them, and the sheep follow him, for they know his voice" (John 10:3-4 ESV).

Paul writes we can better discern the will of God as we are "transformed by the renewal of [our] mind" (Romans 12:2 ESV) and that this is a thoughtful process. "Therefore do not be foolish, but understand what the will of the Lord is" (Ephesians 5:17 ESV).

True to his style, James gives us the whole idea in a nutshell.

Receive with meekness the implanted word, which is able to save your souls.

James 1:21 ESV

This spiritual implanting sounds like something being forced into a place it doesn't belong. But if you ask a gardener, certain factors help cultivate new growth. Primarily, the match cannot be made up of two different species (a cucumber cannot be grafted into a tomato plant). You and I were created in the image of God (Genesis 1:27). We were made with a yearning for God (Psalm 63:1). And Jesus Christ makes the grafting take perfectly. Our responsibility, then, is to receive the Living Word already at work within us. Within you and me lives the power and authority to thwart the very obstacles that seek to destroy us.

The power lives within you to save your soul.

Why would a Christian need to hear this from James? (I thought their souls were already saved?) Because they were clearly not engaging. Instead, they were living powerless lives, bearing little fruit. Defeated. Unproductive. Uncertain of how it could be different.

Take note: It was never meant to be this way.

The life-giving Word of the Gospel message that brought salvation to you as a believer in Christ is the same Living Word that is alive within you. It is this power at work that enables you to "destroy arguments and every lofty opinion raised against the knowledge of God, and take every thought captive to obey Christ" (2 Corinthians 10:5 ESV).

Take a trip to the Mayan ruins at Yucatan, Mexico and you will quickly discover a plant known as the strangler fig. It's a Ficus tree most notorious for causing many of the ruins to be reduced to piles of rubble.[95] By design, the tree sends down its root system, strangling out the nutrients from whatever else is consuming them until it takes over. Birds fed on the figs over time, dropping seeds into the crevices of the walls. Those seeds sprouted, grew, and destroyed the ancient structures.

Our implanted Word can work in our lives just like a strangler fig. There is power to rid yourself of haughty attitudes, selfishness, arrogance, plain ugliness, blatant error, and anything that dishonors the Lord (2 Peter 1:3). If the Word has the power to save your soul, just imagine what it can do for your marriage. For your relationship with your MIL. That hateful neighbor across the street, or for your Monday.

And now I commend you to God and to the word of his grace, which is able to build you up and to give you the inheritance among all those who are sanctified.

Acts 20:32 ESV

BECOMING VIBRANT–

When you and I willingly receive the implanted Word, destroying those thoughts and strongholds that have held us back so long, we will be the most visible version of us in the most beautiful way. And when you find yourself doing this good work, know He is bringing you in. What two ways do you plan to actively receive the implanted Word into your life?

DAY 60:
SAYING GOODBYE TO YOU

Our yielding of ourselves to Him is only possible when we
are quite sure that He has given Himself to us. Our love
which melts us, and bows us in willing, joy-fill surrender,
can only be the echo of His love.

~Alexander MacLaren[96]

I died a slow death to motherhood. My first child arrived just after I started graduate school. The second about two years into it.
Then we relocated to a remote location hundreds of miles away with
years of coursework to complete (without the benefits of Zoom) still
hanging over my tired head. Traveling, data gathering and teaching
at the university balanced out the new role. Some of those first years
are a blur. The oven never needed cleaning and my toddler ate a lot
of Pop-Tarts, but everyone survived. Even though it was difficult, I
was satisfied to be accomplishing what I believed God called me to
do. An added bonus were letters added to my name, pulling me out
of arm candy status (which is the assumption of many as the wife
of a doctor). And in my corner of the world, that distinction was
priceless.

About the time those letters became legit, we picked up Chloe
in China, and my time at the university came to a close. Not once
did I use those letters before hanging up my robe in exchange for
yoga pants and a messy bun. No more statistical analysis, conference
speaking, or suits. I was a full-time mom with three children at home,
caring for a new baby and homeschooling.

Within two years, we added another child who could not speak
English with problems galore. We adopted six children in six years

187

adding to the two biological Stranges in the mix. My coffin was sealed. In terms of the expectations for my life and dreams, this was not it. Cheri Strange was dead.

Turns out, dying was just what I needed to truly live.

Dr. Cheri Strange and what she wanted and needed and thought made her significant needed to die. All of me keeled over in time just the way James describes:

Of his own will he brought us forth by the word of truth, that we should be a kind of firstfruits of his creatures.

James 1:18 ESV

It doesn't make much sense to our western mindset, but this would have a ring of familiarity to the first century Jewish Christians. James harkens back to the Levitical Law involving the first sheaf of the harvest. It was brought into the temple along with a sacrifice on the day after the Passover Sabbath, reminding the people of God's goodness and assuring them of what was yet to come (Leviticus 23:9-14).

What we might miss is that Jesus is the New Testament fulfillment of that practice. He was the literal firstfruit sacrifice on the Passover Sabbath showing us the good that was to come through Him.[97]

When I felt like my dreams were gone and any sense of me forever lost, it came at a time when enough mud had been thrown on my fence to clump together and hold. The Word of Truth was able to speak louder than my own nonsense, enabling me to look beyond the unworn clothes in my closet. The Word of God was there reminding me I was loved. He knew me as a person. And to Him, I loomed large, no matter what I wore or did throughout my days and nights. Of His own will, I am significant to Him and He had plans for my life.

Saying goodbye to me and what I thought I needed to be vibrant and seen was necessary because it reduced my audience to One. The significant One. The One who demonstrated with His life what it looks like to be stripped of self and sense to become a servant of God. And what an audience He is.

The Word of Truth liberates you and me, making us like firstfruits to give those around us a taste of what good can come to them in Jesus. But it cannot happen unless we say goodbye to what we want and think we need and must strive to attain.

I have been crucified with Christ. It is no longer I who live, but Christ who lives in me. And the life I now live in the flesh I live by faith in the Son of God, who loved me and gave himself for me.

Galatians 2:20 ESV

BECOMING VIBRANT–

What does it look like in your life to say goodbye to you and what you think you need to be vibrant and seen? Dying to your dreams and expectations may be what is required for you to truly live. For the days remaining in our journey together, resolve to make Him your sole audience, at least ten minutes a day. Get a journal if that will help. Add Galatians 2:20 to your daily routine until it becomes your reality.

DAY 61:
SAYING HELLO TO TRUE FELLOWSHIP

The physical presence of other Christians is a source of
incomparable joy and strength to the Believer.

~Dietrich Bonhoeffer[98]

What you find as you drive across the Texas countryside is miles
and miles of grazing cows. If you are lucky, you happen upon
an area that has more of the same plus a zebra. Occasionally there
might be a preserve with a handful of the black and white out-of-
place beauties pasturing, but nothing like what exists in Africa. The
Masai Mara reserve located in southwest Kenya hosts one of the largest populations of plains zebras on the planet. Every year between
July and November about 200,000 zebras join up with approximate-
ly 1.5 million wildebeests and thousands of gazelles in the Greater
Serengeti savanna to traverse hundreds of miles together, migrating
southward for food.

Experiencing this phenomenon known as the Great Wildebeest
Migration is unlike anything this side of the Atlantic. I arrived on
African soil carrying this analogy with which you and I are now so
familiar. Mental images emerged of what it is like to become the
proverbial zebra, learning to live within a herd of different animals,
being willing to stand out even if it means being the only one.
But suddenly, on the savanna before me stood thousands of zebras
gathered in one place. Oh, they weren't alone. They were mixed with
hundreds of wildebeests. But together, those black and white beauties
covered the landscape as far as the eye could see. If I hadn't been so
awestruck, I might have burst into tears. Zebras here. Zebras there.
Every day we went out, there were more and more zebras.

Every one unique in their individual DNA, undaunted in confidence, these untamed beings were living the life God designed for them to live. What my eyes beheld wasn't that much different than the zebra scene I carried in my mind, except my image left me feeling lonely. Mylanta! I was alone! My mental picture had been of one zebra, struggling to make it, not a dazzle of them in community. The snapshot I had come to know so well was only part of the whole.

Standing here, the whole picture came into view. Like humans, zebras operate best in community with other zebras. Just like us, they were never created to do life alone. These are social creatures who can live together, in and among herds of certain other animals. And when one of their own is in trouble, hurt, or under threat, the community circles up around them, bringing support and protection they cannot provide for themselves.[99]

It's the same picture we get from the writer of Hebrews:

And let us consider how to stir up one another to love and good works, not neglecting to meet together, as is the habit of some, but encouraging one another, and all the more as you see the Day drawing near.

Hebrews 10:24-25 ESV

Certainly, there are times we find ourselves alone in daily life. You and I feel outnumbered by a different herd. Instead of settling in with an extra helping of loneliness mixed with a side of discouragement, we should recognize we are hardwired for fellowship.

You need me. I need you. In fact, we are responsible for one another. Just like the circle zebras create.

When things were really bad in Macedonia, Paul writes how the coming of Titus gave him and his colleagues comfort (2 Corinthians 7:6). To the church at Philippi, Paul offers gratitude for their long-term partnership in the gospel (Philippians 1:3-5). And in his final letter to Timothy at the end of his life, he urges him to bring Mark, and do it soon (2 Timothy 4:9, 11).

What if we made time for finding other people on the same path? Not that they have to have anything in common with what you like or do for a living. Maybe you have grandkids and she is in her twenties. The person next to her could be an engineer while you teach preschoolers. (God bless you both.) You can be fast friends if you are zebras. Zebras can have nothing else in common but the Holy Spirit and establish a beautiful friendship called fellowship.

> Walking with a friend in the dark is better than walking alone in the light.
>
> ~Helen Keller[100]

BECOMING INVINCIBLE—

Find a small group of women with whom you can associate. Friend people you can encourage and be encouraged by. Meet together with them, living out Hebrews 10:24-25. Start with your local church, for that is where God plants you to grow and minister. If there is nothing available, check out www.sheyearns.com. There you can find daily encouragement and community for exactly this purpose.

Day 62:
Faith Works

A faith which does not fill one's heart with love to God, and
which does not produce a practical sympathy towards one's
fellow-men, is a curious, worthless ... faith.

~C. Jerdan[101]

Becoming vibrant can be messy in daily life. For instance, it means
you and I can no longer learn of a need, assure the person we
will pray for them, and hit them with the non-committal, "If there
is anything I can do . . ." blanket response as we walk away. That, my
friend, is not only unhelpful, it's unbiblical.

It rings with exactly the sort of charity James dismisses as dead
faith, "If a brother or sister is poorly clothed and lacking in daily
food, and one of you says to them, 'Go in peace, be warmed and
filled,' without giving them the things needed for the body, what
good is that? So also faith by itself, if it does not have works, is dead"
(James 2:15-17 ESV).

When James argues for a faith that works, it's not the "saving"
faith of justification Paul writes about (Romans 3:28). The works
you perform cannot get you to a right relationship with God. For
that you need something supernatural: "For by grace you have been
saved through faith. And this is not your own doing; it is the gift of
God" (Ephesians 2:8 ESV). Instead, James takes a practical view of
the issue. If change in your life is real, your faith should be marked
by what you do, not only the words you utter. In other words, your
faith is recognized by the works in your life that come *after* salvation,
not as *the means of* it.[102]

Jesus made the same argument when He told the disciples, "By this all people will know that you are my disciples, if you have love for one another" (John 13:35 ESV). As He explained the relationship between Himself, His Father, and those who believed, He gave a picture of a vine, saying, "By this my Father is glorified, that you bear much fruit and so prove to be my disciples" (John 15:8 ESV). Love and fruit can be seen and often experienced. Jesus is talking about a faith that is evident, like a lamp lighting up a room. Or the call to Go and Show.

At the time of this writing, one of the families in our neighborhood recently contracted Covid-19. The dad was immediately hospitalized with complications. These are parents with jobs, responsibilities, and dreams yet to be realized. The mom cannot be with the dad, and no one can enter the home to help. All she suggested we do is pray and write cards of encouragement, which we all did. Someone mowed the yard, neighbors brought meals, others left gift cards. The birthdays missed while Dad fights for his life were made special. Nothing is being neglected. What I see is faith at work.

The same thing happened to a friend of mine when her son was found to have a terminal brain tumor. Time was short, and all she wanted to do was spend precious moments with him, but there were so many details. Work, other kids and a husband, all hurting. But the body of Christ worked their faith in her life, the life of her family and her son. As she tells it, it was nothing short of blessing. People showed up planting flowers, moving furniture, providing anything God placed in their minds to do, even beyond the time God gave her son on this earth. Even long past the funeral, people sent cards that communicated they knew the hurt lingered long after the child and crises of grief were buried.

Faith *works*. Sometimes your faith working is the only thing that will get a person to the next day, and beyond.

Faith in action is love, and love in action is service. By transforming that faith into living acts of love, we put ourselves in contact with God Himself, with Jesus our Lord.

~Mother Teresa[103]

BECOMING VIBRANT—

Will you ask the Lord to show you how you can work your faith? To the one you least expect? In your neighborhood? This week. Even today.

DAY 63:
BEYOND THE CAFETERIA

*Religion that is pure and undefiled before God the Father is
this: to visit orphans and widows in their affliction, and to
keep oneself unstained from the world.*

James 1:27 ESV

Sometimes God will ask you and I to move beyond the needs of our
neighbor or our friends. Exceeding the high school lunch table,
God will move us out to show light and love to those in the world
who are shunned, overlooked and even abused by others. That's what
James is getting at in his call to *"pure and undefiled religion."*

Maybe it will begin with a thought or a burden. It might seem
irrational to imagine you could do anything. Still, the twinge in your
heart remains until you take action. That's what James has in mind
when he called people to visit widows and orphans. True religion
requires looking beyond yourself, getting involved in the struggle,
and looking after the most vulnerable in our society.[104] The calling is
not limited to a mission trip or a Go Fund Me campaign. Don't get
me wrong. We need those. God means for us to go further and do
more than fits our comfort level on behalf of the needy or oppressed
today.

I was nineteen, sitting in World History my second year of
college. The professor mentioned the one-child policy in China and
the resulting orphan crisis where babies, particularly girls, were being
abandoned. Of all the historical information I let drain from my
brain those years, that burden stayed with me into marriage, through
two biological children, and three college degrees. I never intended to
do anything more than stay in my lane, living my average Christian

life. But God did not let me give up that burden. Instead, He used it to change lives, including my own.

God moved in the life of Amy Carmichael in a similar way. Born in Ireland in 1867, Amy spent her young life near the mill her father owned. As a young woman, she became burdened for the girls who worked in the mills to know the Lord. These girls were poor nobodies. Amy, the owner's daughter, started a class just for these women that grew to serve five hundred women.[105]

In no time at all, Amy found herself led by the Lord to the mission field in India. One day, a little girl ran into the missionary compound begging for protection. She revealed she was sold by her parents to the gods for temple prostitution, and there were many others like her. Once Amy caught wind of what was happening, she could not let it go.

Much like the burden for her girls at the mill, she took action, regardless of the danger and threats. Amy began strategically rescuing girls, to care for and educate them. This became her mission, so that eventually in her ministry to India, she rescued one thousand children, both girls and boys.

It is a safe thing to trust Him to fulfill the desires which He creates.

~Amy Carmichael[106]

BECOMING VISIBLE—

Do you have a God-given burden? A desire? A twinge in your heart that breaks over an injustice toward the most vulnerable? God is still on the move using people like you, and hopelessly average Christian girls like me, to change the world. What will He have you do?

DAY 64:
MERCY WINS

The Gospel is good news of mercy to the undeserving. The
symbol of the religion of Jesus is the cross, not the scales.

~John Stott[107]

No one came to my party. At least not the ones I expected. And I wasn't seven years old. It was an adult-y shindig. This event wasn't the first and it wouldn't be the last time people close to me didn't show up when it mattered. Often these occasions simply add to the "you're no one special" wallflower narrative. Raising six daughters and fifteen years of ministry tells me people haven't shown up for you when you most needed them, either.

The unimportant, invisible me was hurt and critical when these situations occurred. The insult cut deeply and lasted a long time. But the failing forward, more vibrant version of myself recognizes— she has disappointed a few people herself. And when the same thing happens again, because it will, this present version of me finds great wisdom in the advice Paul offers Timothy about these matters.

*For Demas, in love with this present world, has deserted
me and gone to Thessalonica. Crescens has gone to Galatia,
Titus to Dalmatia. Luke alone is with me. Get Mark and
bring him with you, for he is very useful to me for ministry.
Tychicus I have sent to Ephesus.*

2 Timothy 4:10-12 ESV

Paul spends a whole section outlining the ins and outs of his lonely predicament, and when it couldn't get any worse, adds, "At my first defense no one came to stand by me, but all deserted me." His best advice to Timothy is, "May it not be held against them!" (2 Timothy 4:16 ESV).

Paul wants Timothy to know relationships are hard. People disappoint and let you down. But you cannot allow their hurtful choices and actions to mark you. Forgiveness is needed. He has learned through his own mud-slinging adventures something he wants the reader to learn as well.

Mercy triumphs over judgment.

James 2:13 ESV

First, we learn Paul's good friends are gone, and he doesn't explain why. A variety of things can occur, keeping good friends from showing up for us. Maybe what Paul is not saying is just as important as what he is saying? They just couldn't be there, and they are still in his circle. Where you and I want to write them off, as might Timothy as well, Paul offers a different approach.

Then there was Demas. Note this man is included in the greetings in two of Paul's other letters (Colossians 4:14 and Philemon 1:24). A trusted friend and colleague, Demas was a believer who left. He left Paul in the lurch, high and dry. Why? We don't know. What we need to take from this personal insider information is how tempting temptation can be to a zebra. Even a close comrade of the Apostle Paul can fall out of love with Jesus for what will never satisfy and leave it all behind.

Paul leaves this piece of himself on the page for us to know the departure of Demas broke his heart. The task for you and I to go around doing our daily To-Do List while keeping heaven in our hearts is not for the cowardly.[108] It is possible to come in close and still turn away. So Paul, compelled by compassion, writes not to hold it against him.

In these messy situations, one thread runs throughout—relationships are hard, and when they are, let mercy win.

Be merciful, even as your Father is merciful.

Luke 6:36 ESV

BECOMING VIBRANT—

Is there someone you need to extend mercy toward? A friend or family member you have "written off" because they let you down when you most needed them? Again? I know it's excruciating. Lonely. And not right. But Paul is right. *Let it not be held against them.* It's your vibrancy at stake, and possibly theirs.

DAY 65:
FAILING FORWARD FEAT #7

The more we focus on who we are in Christ, the less it matters
who we were in the past, or even what happened to us.

~Joyce Meyer[109]

On October 5, 1994, all the little girls around the world familiar
with the tale found themselves swimming in a pool of disappointment. On this date, scientists uncovered a great mystery many
would have rather left mysterious. Researchers discovered Anna Anderson, a woman who died a decade earlier, was not who she claimed
to be. Normally, no one would care, but this mysterious woman
claimed to be the long-lost Russian princess, Anastasia.[110]

Anastasia was the youngest daughter of Russian Czar Nicholas
II. The Bolsheviks ordered the whole family executed in 1918 during
the Russian Revolution. Something went awry as shots were fired,
causing bullets to ricochet off the walls. None of the bodies were
recovered. Rumors of possible survivors began to spread. Two years
later, a young woman showed up in a German mental hospital,
refusing to reveal her identity. Still a patient, she saw a headline in a
magazine about the lost princess and began to reveal she was the girl
for whom they were looking.[111]

The truth is that Anna Anderson was not even Anna Anderson.
Her name is Franziska Schanzkowski, a Polish farm worker. Her
whole life was a sham. Franziska fabricated her identity over time
based upon stories she heard, customs she learned, information she
gleaned from visitors, paying attention to tips and tricks picked up
from others to make her role convincing. And it was, to her death
and beyond.

Anna Anderson's tale is discouraging because we want to believe the fairytale. Beauty from ashes, pauper to princess. It's in our DNA. But honestly, I think, at the same time, we are afraid if it happened to us, it would turn out to be a sham. No matter how much we want the fairytale to be true for us, it just can't be. Somehow, we will be bamboozled.

Those reading the letter from James were doing some questioning of their own.

Listen, my beloved brothers, has not God chosen those who are poor in the world to be rich in faith and heirs of the kingdom, which he has promised to those who love him?

James 2:5 ESV

As believers in Christ, regardless of worldly status, culture, family structure, or zip code, our identity is changed. Paul writes that "because we are his children, God has sent the Spirit of his Son into our hearts, prompting us to call out, 'Abba, Father.' Now you are no longer a slave but God's own child. And since you are his child, God has made you his heir" (Galatians 4:6-7 NLT).

As heirs, we become *rich in faith* and *heirs of the kingdom*. James is reminding his readers that they are living a genuine, never-ending fairytale. But how can a person embrace this identity? What does this mean for a girl accustomed to keeping her head down, living with all kinds of hurts and disappointment?

Take a lesson from Franziska Schanzkowski. She took every opportunity to learn and embrace her new identity. From how to talk, what to know, who to avoid, to what to embrace, Franziska was lost forever. Old habits gone for good to make room for the new. She made the choice to embrace her new identity, leaving what was in the past behind her.

You, my friend, are an heir of the kingdom. You are rich in faith. There is no tale that is more *forever after* than yours.

Forget your own people also, and your father's house; So the King will greatly desire your beauty; Because He is your Lord, worship Him.

Psalm 45:10-11 NKJV

BECOMING VIBRANT—

A daughter of the King knows who she is and lives out her days in the security of that knowing. Learn these realities about yourself. Then think about how believing them will help you live out your days differently. What should a princess who is loved by the King do?

1 Corinthians 6:11

1 Peter 1:4

Ephesians 1:3-4

Ephesians 1:7-11

Ephesians 2:5-7

PART V
CHAPTER 8

HOW TO BECOME INVINCIBLE

There is a story in the Old Testament, of a vision given to Ezekiel the prophet at a time when life had been devastating and difficult. The people of God, living in Jerusalem, had disobeyed and followed everything but God for generations. When He could endure their wickedness no longer, God brought judgment using the Babylonians. Consequently, death and destruction, along with famine and loss become commonplace. You can imagine what this catastrophe did to the outlook on the future for the survivors.

It was hopeless. They felt abandoned, forgotten, and alone. They were utterly lifeless.

God takes Ezekiel out of town to a valley filled with dry bones. In fact, they were "very dry" (Ezekiel 37:2), meaning those they represent have been dead a long time. As Ezekiel moves around the bones, God asks one question, "Son of man, can these bones live?" Ezekiel answers wisely, "Lord GOD, only you know" (Ezekiel 37:3 CSB).

Then God does something incredible. He instructs Ezekiel to speak to the bones, putting flesh on them and breath in them, making them into a living, breathing army. At this time, God reminds Ezekiel the people have been saying, "Our bones are dried up, and our hope has perished" (Ezekiel 37:11 CSB). But God shows the prophet He can make dead people live again, as a picture of what He promises to do for His hurting people.

I will put my Spirit in you, and you will live, and I will settle you in your own land. Then you will know that I am the LORD. I have spoken, and I will do it. This is the declaration of the LORD."

Ezekiel 37:14 CSB

God makes the lifeless live again.

As miraculous as taking a pile of bones and turning them into a stunning human being with soul, worth, and personality is, this is His specialty. God makes dead people alive again. A plan of any variety on its own merit will never get you there. The only path to invincible is through dry bones made alive. Once He puts His Spirit in you—nothing can hinder what He wants you to become. You and I participate in the journey.

You can become the most uninhibited, confident, and immovable version of you. Such renovation of the heart, mind, and soul doesn't happen overnight. Most of the time it is a process. These final readings help illuminate what is possible and necessary for a woman who has been left out, lonely, familiar with lifeless dry bones to participate in becoming who she longs to be.

DAY 66:
WHAT TO AIM TOWARD

Take the world, but give me Jesus;

In His cross my trust shall be,

Till, with clearer, brighter vision

Face to face my Lord I see.

~Fanny Crosby [112]

A plan does not help if it fails to propel the person toward the ultimate goal. What does it look like to live in such a way that you are seen by others to the glory of God? How do you shine a light on what is dark, living beyond what once limited you and kept you hidden in the shadows?

We need to know what we are aiming toward, day to day. When the final page is turned and it's just you, what should you do? Do you know what to pursue? Once again, our guide, James, offers some sound advice about daily life as one Going and Showing as he nears the end of his letter. The message is just what you and I need as we look ahead to tomorrow.

The Christians were going about their daily business without thinking about or consulting what the Lord might desire in their lives. It's not that they were conducting any type of business that was questionable or ungodly. These were ordinary moral industrious businessmen.[113] The problem was deeper. They were separating their day to day living from their religion.

Come now, you who say, "Today or tomorrow we will go into
such and such a town and spend a year there and trade and make
a profit"—yet you do not know what tomorrow will bring.

James 4:13-14 ESV

These individuals were failing to incorporate who Jesus was making them to be, into the ins and outs of regular living. He was a compartment in their lives they could open and close. And the issue James raises is equally problematic. Not only were they not thinking about Jesus in the present, He wasn't a factor in their future.

What is your life? For you are a mist that appears for a little
time and then vanishes. Instead you ought to say, "If the Lord
wills, we will live and do this or that."

James 4:14-15 ESV

James is chiding them a bit when he tells them they should say, *"If the Lord wills."* It's not a phrase that guarantees blessing or anything magical. The phrase was common. Nonbelievers used it in conversation, sort of like, *"If the sun's still shining."*[14] The point is not that they should slap those particular words in front of every possible option for what they might do, but that it appears the Lord is not even on their minds.

The call to you and to me is to place every aspect of life before the Lord, rather than close Him up behind a door somewhere. Your God deeply cares about your ordinary life activities. And He wants to be an integral aspect, not a spectator.

For we are His workmanship [His own master work, a
work of art], created in Christ Jesus [reborn from above—
spiritually transformed, renewed, ready to be used] for good
works, which God prepared [for us] beforehand [taking paths

which He set], so that we would walk in them [living the good life which He prearranged and made ready for us].

Ephesians 2:10 AMP

BECOMING INVINCIBLE–

This whole chapter is going to continue helping us catch a better glimpse of what we should be aiming toward. The first element is to ensure the Lord is a key player in our everyday pursuits. As you reflect on your own temperament, your habits, and where you are today, what do you need to do to make the Lord a more fundamental part of your day? How do you think this will impact what you aim toward?

Day 67:
Bleeding Black and White

May the Holy Spirit quicken us, raise our courage,
strengthen our faith, and confirm our confidence in him
while we think on what God has done and is doing in the
midst of his church. Valiantly has the Lord worked for us
and in us; and he will also do great things by us.

~Charles H. Spurgeon[115]

Between my sophomore and junior years in college I served as a summer missionary in South Dakota. Our primary responsibility was singing patriotic music at Mount Rushmore and ministering to traveling families. But we spent one week in Sturgis.

Sturgis, South Dakota is a national phenomenon as the annual location of the largest biker rally in the country. A motley crew, for sure, we were there to take blood pressure, hand out free water, and show the love of Jesus while blending into the wall as much as possible. (No problem.)

As the fiftieth reunion with an unprecedented number of participants, it was an unbelievable site. All the shopkeepers rent out their storefronts and leave town for the two weeks, while thousands of visitors sport their leather wears, bushy beards, and exposed tattoos (this, of course, before tattoos and beards were cool).

After a few days of offering our services as people rumbled and romped through the streets, the truth became clear. Many bikers were just dressing the part. These were largely insurance salesmen, teachers, and entrepreneurs on vacation—not Hells Angels members ready to kill someone in the street. These people bike to Sturgis, sporting their badness, looking the rough and tough biker-dude part. *But that wasn't who they are.*

Becoming the zebra is not like going to Sturgis for vacation. You can't just look the part. You can't decide to be a zebra like selecting a hobby or a team to support. There is no slapping on your leather, hopping on your Harley for a few days, all to be hung in the closet and parked in the garage when you return home. What we are moving toward doesn't work that way. It's an all-in transformation taking place from the inside out until you experience such radical change you practically bleed black and white.

That's what we would say today about diehard fans of something, isn't it, when they take on the very essence of who and what team they adore? We could call James, John the Baptist, and Paul diehard fans in today's vernacular. *He must increase, you must decrease* lived out in the flesh is more striking than anything else John could have declared. Paul, whose life looks much the same in the pursuit of Christlikeness, wrote, "to live is Christ, and to die is gain" (Philippians 1:21 ESV). If the colors for Team Jesus are marked like a zebra, these men bled black and white. They did not simply take a road trip or wear a uniform. Being the zebra was the only way to live, regardless of the cost.

What does it look like for former wallflower nobodies, once weighed down by loads of misguided understandings and years of loneliness and hurt hidden deep inside, to bleed black and white?

As citizens of heaven, live your life worthy of the gospel of Christ.

Philippians 1:27 CSB

No longer are you lost to petty estimations of your worth. When you are not included, it stings, but it does not devastate. If you get passed over, it might be crushing, but you will not be destroyed. Your newfound strength of character is not because you are All That. You have thrown enough mud onto your fence to possess an understanding of who you are—that you possess something more precious than suitcases of misguided understandings, healing years of hidden hurts, and giving worth where there was none.

Therefore, if anyone is in Christ, he is a new creation. The old has passed away; behold, the new has come.

2 Corinthians 5:17 ESV

BECOMING INVINCIBLE—

If you want to be done with all that has torn you up on the insides, left you lonely, and kept you in the corner, become a diehard fan. More than. Leave Sturgis and live your life worthy of the gospel of Christ. Bleed black and white, Sister. It's the only path to invincible. What is one way you can make this your reality today?

Day 68:
Becoming Invincible

Darkness comes. In the middle of it, the future looks blank.
The temptation to quit is huge. Don't. You are in good
company . . . You will argue with yourself that there is no
way forward. But with God, nothing is impossible. He has
more ropes and ladders and tunnels out of pits than you can
conceive. Wait. Pray without ceasing. Hope.

~John Piper[116]

Our puppies grow into dogs. I don't know what happens at your
house, but those cute little fluff balls chew so many bones and
leg posts they gain ninety more pounds. After a year of containing
our indoor giants, we decided something needed to give. A fence for
the backyard. That's what we needed. Easy, right? Not exactly. It took
three different contractors to get it approved, and months more to
have it installed because of the guidelines given by our HOA. The
contract required concrete pillars that anchor the fence panels at least
five feet underground. At the time, it seemed costly and ridiculous.
Why the fuss? Last week, the fuss became obvious.

Right on schedule, in the height of hurricane season, one made
landfall in our area. We are just a few feet above sea level, and the
same distance from the shore. With the rains come tumultuous
winds. Winds that blow stuff down. Stuff that's not anchored well.

When most people around us were making all sorts of repairs
or replacing structures entirely, nothing in my neighborhood was
disturbed. Not a single splinter displaced because our foundation is
secure.

Where does the confidence to live beyond your personality, in spite of your circumstances, and above public and private opinion arise? Your consciousness is no help. A list of accomplishments or a lack thereof will not do the trick. You and I need something more lasting and surer on which to anchor our mud-enriched fence-posts. A force that goes deep so that when the hurricane-like forces of life arise, we are unmoved.

This journey has been answering that question. Even when we feel unwanted by others, lonely, or overlooked, God sees us, He knows us personally, and He does not hold such opinions of our worth. Instead, He bids us to see differently and therefore live differently, Going and Showing who He is through our own personalities, which He finds striking. But we can only do this when we wholly depend on Him in the absolute Truth of the Bible. These components guide us as we move and grow and develop into a zebra-like contrast to the world around us. But there is more.

> *... even as he chose us in him before the foundation of the world, that we should be holy and blameless before him. In love he predestined us for adoption to himself as sons through Jesus Christ, according to the purpose of his will, to the praise of his glorious grace, with which he has blessed us in the Beloved.*

Ephesians 1:4-6 ESV

You visited these verses back on Day 26 when we discovered our personal inheritance as heirs of the King. Wrapped up in the lavishness of heavenly blessing is sovereignty that cannot be thwarted. My course is set. The destination is determined, with the timeline and events written and established (as is yours). God can use any road to bring us to Himself, accomplishing anything He desires. Nothing is wasted. Not even our wanderings or our failings are pointless.

When you and I begin to live in this reality, we become spiritually *invincible*, immovable in our faith. Throwing mud at a chainlinked fence until you can no longer see through it gives deep roots to what you believe and to whom you belong, so that whether the Lord changes the circumstances or chooses to leave them undisrupted for the next thirty years, you and I are secure. Either way, the herd in our midst does not thwart who God determines you and me to be and what He calls us to do.

He only is my rock and my salvation, my fortress; I shall not be shaken.

Psalm 62:6 ESV

BECOMING INVINCIBLE—

You shall not be shaken. Write this truth on your heart and mind as a constant reminder. Then write it where you can see it. The Lord is sovereign over your life. In Him, you are immovable.

DAY 69:
She Did What She Could

You have been created by God and for God, and someday
you will stand amazed at the simple yet profound ways He
has used you even when you weren't aware of it.

~Kay Arthur[117]

When people look at me from the outside, I can give the impression I am a confident, grab-the-bull-by-the-horns-type go-getter. What else would I be with all the education and children I didn't have to have?

You know that can't be right. It must be something else—some other motivation to cause me to do what I don't believe I can and risk what I cannot possess. Then what made the difference?

I have simply learned to walk in the dark. God has given me ample opportunities to believe Him and choose to trust Him. Then I take the next step into what I cannot see. That is how I came to be a mom of eight beautifully diverse children. In fact, walking in the dark is how most everything fruitful and worthwhile has entered my life.

But I haven't always been willing to take that step into the haze of the unknown. Sometimes I have known, like Jonah, and sailed myself in the other direction. Other times, I just made myself too busy to meet the need, make the call, or fill the spot. Then there are those crazy ideas in my head that pop up from time to time. Weird possibilities. Is it the Holy Spirit or my creativity run amuck? Maybe it's gas? Most of the time, I decide on the latter, figuring no one wants my wallflower ideas.

Honestly, it's been those gassy screwball ideas that have fed my fortitude. For example, there have been times when I made too much food and driven it to someone's house unannounced, only to have the person greet me with a bear hug and tears, whispering, "How did you know?" There have been days when I suddenly think of a particular person and at the same time, an item comes to mind. When I meet that person the next time, I find it is exactly what they need. These instances are matched with failures when I have not heeded my harebrained ideas, only to learn a need was not met at the exact time they came to my mind.

This mental nudging and these seeming coincidences are all the work of the Holy Spirit aligning His people for doing His work. I recognize it now. Often these nudgings seem like interruptions to my day and my own agenda. I think this might be why James urges us to see our not following through for what it is: sin.

So whoever knows the right thing to do and fails to do it, for him it is sin.

James 4:17 ESV

When we decided to take those steps in the dark toward adopting a sibling set of four older kids from another country, I knew it was the right thing to do. For me, the nudging came the same way from the Holy Spirit and from the Word of God as those other crazy ideas I once brushed off as something disagreeable I had eaten for dinner. But this time, it was my life at stake. My entire future. Everything we had worked toward financially and the roots we had established—all at risk.

What if the way forward is oh so very dim, and you don't know how it's going to turn out? Is it still sin not to do good when so much is at stake?

In 2018, all international adoptions ceased in Ethiopia. Our adoption was finalized before the door shut. Unknown to us at the time, it was a window of opportunity *to know the right thing and to do it.* In 2019 I witnessed the calamities and costs other girls orphaned in the same city at the same time and of the same ages as my kids are now experiencing. I know it wasn't gas.

Mark writes of a moment in time when a woman enters a room where Jesus is dining with Simon the leper and religious people (Mark 14:1-9). She is there for one purpose: to pour perfume on the feet of Jesus. Now that's a crazy idea. It would have been everything she was worth. Her actions cost her fiscally, socially and emotionally. To pour perfume on a living person was not normal, and to wipe it up with her hair, unparalleled.

What does Jesus say about her hair-brained idea?

She did what she could.

Mark 14:8 NIV

BECOMING INVINCIBLE—

Take note of the nudgings, the ideas that sound crazy, those little notions that are so easy to bat down and discredit as wallflower nothingness. Let me encourage you to start acting on these. Test them. If it's indigestion, you will know. But if it's the Holy Spirit, you will not want to miss it. Is there anything you should act upon today? Let it be said of you and me, "It wasn't conventional or praiseworthy, but she did what she could." Do what you can while it can be done.

Day 70:
Few Good-Friendedness

You adulterous people! Do you not know that friendship with the world is enmity with God? Therefore whoever wishes to be a friend of the world makes himself an enemy of God.

James 4:4 ESV

Sometimes I think James has actually been privy to the middle school locker room scene. Once again, he hits on an issue that has come through my house, my youth group, my ministry, and in my own life over and over again. It goes something like this: the friend group you want to be a part of, for whatever reason, does not find you or me to meet the qualifications on our own, so we must try to prove our coolness to them. We bend, we bow, we put on our cutest t-shirts—all to get that status of belonging, feeling a part, and finding our groove within the majority.

There is always a cost to pursuing coolness. There is always a compromise, and it rests on you. If you want to be a part of the herd of everyone else, there are certain things to which you must adhere and others you must let go.

In regular life, it looks like fitting in at the lunch table, receiving an invitation to the party, being included in the group chat, acceptance in the circle of conversation when you arrive, or space being made for you at the event all are attending together. What we want to avoid is being excluded from the group chat, ignored when we show up, closed off from an available spot at the lunch table, and denied a ticket to the group event.

Can I please issue a memo that may be worth the price of this book?

218

To: The girl trying to be included with the group

From: The friend you wish you always had

Memo:

> Your groove will not be found fitting in with the majority.

> Any relationship in which you need to perform to gain access is toxic.

> The cool people friend group (or anything like it) is toxic for a believer.

> Attempts to fit in with the majority will only hurt you.

When I was a child, my favorite scary movie was *The Creature from the Black Lagoon*. Spoiler alert, it's a black and white film in which a man, obviously dressed up in a lizard-like costume, steals the beautiful girl from a ship until she is rescued by the handsome hero. Okay, maybe I'm incredulous because of the technology available today, but it's quite obvious the villain is merely a man dressed up in a lizard-like costume, pretending to be something he's not.

The same is true for you and me when we move toward relationships that reflect the world more than they imitate Jesus. We fool no one. It's not just me who offers an awesome illustration for how striking you look against the rest of humanity. "You are the light of the world. A city set on a hill cannot be hidden" (Matthew 5:14 ESV). Everyone knows you are a zebra trying to put on a cow costume. It's not convincing when you do. Disaster only awaits.

Take a second memo.

To: The girl afraid of being left alone without a friend

From: The friend you may never know personally

Memo:

You will be okay if stand out. Don't worry or feel sad when you are not missed by the cute t-shirt settlers. Use spiritual eyes to see white stripes instead of black ones. Ask God for the ability to see people who need a friend. She is out there, friendless, just like you. Maybe she's not so cool. Likely there is someone needing a friend, feeling friendless. Be willing to be a friend to the uncool, the unpopular, the unnoticed, albeit another lone zebra. Most of the time, she will be a most loyal companion, the best listener, and more serious about the Lord.

Don't leave your relationships to chance. Pray for godly people to come into your life with whom you can connect. Don't force relationships to happen. Pray for them to happen. Then when they do, nurture them with prayer.

~Stormie Omartian[118]

BECOMING VIBRANT—

Take to heart James 4:4. Pray about your friendships and let God orchestrate them as He wills. May God open your eyes to see those He wants you to befriend.

.

Day 71:
Work Your Prayers

He who kneels the most, stands the best.

~D.L. Moody[119]

Friday, the outside of our house was power-washed to pristine perfection. The siding and brick were sparkling white. The sidewalks and stairway spotless (HOA requirements). That was four days ago. Before the category 1 hurricane blew through our area. Today, it's a real mess outside. Nothing to call in aid workers or the insurance company about. Just work. We didn't even move anything off the back porch. In fact, we turned off the lights and went to bed, like nothing was going on. At this point in our coastal history, a category 1 hurricane is ordinary life. We will spend the next days cleaning up debris, collecting limbs, and repairing details on the property. As I look out my back windows, I am reminded how experience shapes our perspective.

As James begins to close out his letter, he throws in a quick reminder about prayer.

Is anyone among you suffering? Let him pray. Is anyone cheerful? Let him sing praises. Is anyone among you sick? Let him call for the elders of the church, and let them pray over him, anointing him with oil in the name of the Lord.

James 5:13-14 ESV

Yes. Some days will be filled with sheer awesomeness. The kids are doing well. Maybe you get an unexpected raise. Everyone is healthy. Even the dog minds. Other times, you and I can shine our light. Sport our stripes. Do everything right. Still, gloomy days wrought with disappointments come. Setbacks show up uninvited. Problems exceed our ability to solve them. We won't have enough or be enough. And then someone gets sick, turning the realm of what was normal upside down.

I'm guessing James knows our immediate response when things get hairy is not to pray. Curse, maybe. Cry a bit. Call a friend. Sulk. Eat a package of Oreos. Medicate. Take it out on our family and co-workers, most definitely. Still. After all we have learned. Even with the forward failing adventures, we can get caught up in the drama, allowing ourselves to become exasperated rather than taking our concerns first to God.

He's right. Some days will be like looking outside in the light of day after a hurricane. Yesterday, all was well. Praise God in the goodness. But more effective than cursing or stewing the hours away because the world has turned on its head, is prayer. Pray in the middle of the mess. Pray because prayer works. And if you can't pray because of illness or you have no strength,[120] call on the elders to pray for you. The point is to draw upon the power of the One you trust.

James is not questioning whether his coming to God will help or if he will be heard. Nor does he hold back the ordinary ups and downs life brings. Bring all of it. And when you can't, enlist people who can. Trust your all to the Lord.

How does a man who did not believe come to possess such deeply convincing conviction? We can't know the answer with certainty, but we can glean a lot from his habits. Tradition holds James was found so often on his knees praying, his knees became hardened. People called him "Camel Knees,"[121] living out what he proclaims to you and me.

I wonder, if James were standing before us, urging us to petition in the down times, praise on the good days, and call in reinforcements when we can't find the strength ourselves, if my eyes would be focused on anything other than the man's knees.

The power of a praying woman does not depend on what she can do with her own hands, but in the mighty Hand of God.

~Gift Guru Mona[122]

BECOMING INVINCIBLE–

There is nothing magical about our praying posture, but when my knees are involved, my words and actions are more focused. In essence, I work my prayers more effectively, losing that laissez-faire attitude that crops up as if I'm not talking to the King. Today, if your body can bear it, find a spot in your house to kneel. Meet God in that posture as often as you can.

DAY 72:
CONSIDERING IMPOSSIBLE POSSIBILITIES

Be wretched and mourn and weep. Let your laughter
be turned to mourning and your joy to gloom. Humble
yourselves before the Lord, and he will exalt you.

James 4:9-10 ESV

Chances are, you are not famous. Likely, you have fewer than a million followers on any platform, and you're not booked as the main attraction for the year. Those possibilities may not even be appealing to you, but consider for a moment that God might have something for you lying beyond what you can imagine. Impossible possibilities are His way of working through His people.

Whenever God has done a mighty work it has been by some
very insignificant instrument.

~Charles H. Spurgeon[123]

Remember Hannah? She was insignificant. One of two wives, she was childless until she prayed in her desperation and dependence upon God. Ruth, the Moabite woman, also ranked as socially insignificant, being a foreigner and widow. But God pieced her life together, granting her lineage in the line of David. He did the same thing with a nobody harlot named Rahab from Jericho.

In case there is a temptation to claim God worked one way in the times of the Bible and another in present day history, let's take a more recent example. George Whitfield may not be a household name, but he is considered the first American celebrity and largely responsible for the Great Awakening on both sides of the Atlantic.

In short, great things were not expected from Whitfield. He was poor and lost. But at college, he met the Wesley brothers (founders of the Methodist Church),[124] became a believer, and started preaching. His style matched his gifting in theater and dramatics. Instead of pastoring a church, he became an itinerant preacher, traveling around with one objective—that people hear the Gospel and be transformed by it. It is estimated that in his lifetime, he preached 1,000 times per year for thirty years, bringing untold millions to Christ.[125]

I recognize you are not a George Whitfield. Still, you do qualify as an "insignificant instrument." No less. What God envisioned for me required a personal death and resurrection, part of which I have already shared. A death, not only to my personal wants and desires, but to my vision of what I *could not become*.

There were internal flashes of what I thought were hokey dreams or misdirected aims that pointed me toward my skills as a writer and ability to communicate in person. I dismissed them as far-fetched longings, like wanting to become an Olympic figure skater or a winner on *The Voice*—possibilities out of my league, training, experience, and lot in life. It was beyond arrogant. The mere entertainment of the thought I could do what I'm doing today was ludicrous. (I wasn't even asked to teach a Sunday School class, give my testimony, or lead a prayer.)

If you have discovered over these days how much your God loves you, desires for you to come in closer, and how firm is his unfailing grace, then you know what James means when he says, "humble yourselves before the Lord," (James 4:10 ESV). God's specialty is working wonders through the likes of you and me. My friend, are you willing to give up your own vision of what *cannot be true* for you? Are you ready to let God decide what impossibilities are impossible in your life and which ones you were made for?

Now all glory to God, who is able, through his mighty power at work within us, to accomplish infinitely more than we might ask or think.

Ephesians 3:20 NLT

BECOMING INVINCIBLE—

Do you have a vision of something you feel God might have you do, yet all evidence is to the contrary? Maybe it's a kooky idea, even to you. I don't need to be impressed with your dream. Neither do you. The vision is God's to do something mighty through your life. If you know, write down what impossible possibility you think God is calling you toward.

Day 73:
Wait Well

Waiting on God requires the willingness to bear uncertainty,
to carry within oneself the unanswered question, lifting
the heart to God about it whenever it intrudes upon one's
thoughts.

~Elisabeth Elliot[126]

Maybe your circumstances have not yet changed. I get it. In some environments, I am still unknown as a person, yet accounted for based on someone else's status. Sometimes, not even that. Not long ago, we received a package addressed to my husband and *someone else*. A few weeks later, at another informal gathering, my spouse was introduced to the room while I was invited to stand in the too-unimportant-to-mention awkwardness as the only other adult in the room. It still happens. Even though I no longer cling to the wallpaper or find my identity in who or what they call me or don't call me, I wish it were different.

You likely feel the same about people and situations in your life. We can relate so well to David in his longing for God to move in the lives of those who hurt him. What if it's thirty years? I know that's not the question you want, but it might need to be right here. Suppose nothing outside of yourself changes? What then?

Be patient, therefore, brothers, until the coming of the Lord.
See how the farmer waits for the precious fruit of the earth,
being patient about it, until it receives the early and the

late rains. You also, be patient. Establish your hearts, for the
coming of the Lord is at hand.

James 5:7-8 ESV

It's as if James is answering our difficult question, "What if nothing outside of ourselves changes?" His response is not what comes naturally. *You also, be patient.* The idea of patience found in verse seven brings "an element of suffering due to other people."[127] My knee-jerk reaction is to take matters into my own hands, ruminating over the comeback I wish I had said, or rehearsing my words for the next clash. James proposes exhibiting endurance with our difficult people without complaining.[128]

Have you ever lived or worked on a small independent farm? These are my father's roots. Forty acres, complete with an original buffalo wallow from when buffalo roamed the plains. It was a life of dependence. The future state of the family rested on the incoming crop. When all the reserves were spent, the last few weeks before the harvest brought meager meals with some suffering. They awaited the rains, hoping for timely showers. One bad year could be disastrous. The farmer must be patient, hungry or well fed, waiting for the harvest God will bring.[129]

Everyone under the sun waits. The question is not, "Are you going to wait?" But, "Are you going to <u>wait well</u>?" Are you and I going to walk firmly in our faith, no matter how long the difficulty persists, without giving up the pursuit to become invincible?

Wait for the LORD; be strong, and let your heart take
courage; wait for the LORD!

Psalm 27:14 ESV

BECOMING INVINCIBLE—

More than anything, you and I need to remember waiting well doesn't mean sitting around doing nothing. The farmer is never idle. Neither is the lover of Jesus. Here are five things we can do to navigate waiting well:

1. Cling to the Father (like Hannah), even when it feels like He is not listening.

2. Ask for help to navigate a way forward when you can't see the path (2 Chronicles 20:12).

3. Trust His record. Recall all the times God has come through for you in the past. And if you can't, trust His character. Scripture can show you who He is and why He is reliable (Exodus 34:6-7; 1 John 4:8; Isaiah 40:28; Micah 7:18-19).

4. Before anything right happens, rejoice in His promise to fulfill in you His purpose for your life (2 Chronicles 20:20-22).

5. Be ready for the harvest to come in, because He will not, will not, fail you (Hebrews 13:5).

DAY 74:
BECOMING UNMOVABLE

Behold, we consider those blessed who remained steadfast.
You have heard of the steadfastness of Job, and you have seen
the purpose of the Lord, how the Lord is compassionate and
merciful.

James 5:11 ESV

It's one thing to sit in my kitchen with everything right in the world and write about becoming steadfast and unmovable. I can courageously be encouraged to embark on my calling and the great purpose in life God has given to me. But it's quite another in the face of uncertainty, with troubles enumerated. When more loss than a person should bear has come, all I hold dear has been destroyed, and the doctors decide the only outlook for my future is a sure and painful death. To say then, without a tremor in my voice, or a slight hesitation, "None of these move me, if I can only do what my Father has called me to do"—is to be invincible.

But none of these things move me, neither count I my life
dear unto myself, so that I might finish my course with joy,
and the ministry, which I have received of the Lord Jesus, to
testify the gospel of the grace of God.

Acts 20:24 KJV

What if I don't find myself today in dire straits, alone in a jail cell awaiting execution like Paul, or given a lethal diagnosis? Suppose I am living a life with normal ups and downs in suburbia or downtown in a metropolis? Am I out of luck in terms of becoming invincible? Is *perfect and complete* reserved for the super Christians after all?

No. Becoming invincible is not what happens in the heat of the moment like we suddenly put on a super suit. It's a gradual development, like covering a chainlinked fence with mud. We might view it like an intentional road we walk to become more intimately acquainted with Jesus, much like becoming the zebra version of ourselves. Becoming invincible is the quality needed in the ordinary good days so that when trouble comes and the bottom falls out of your life, you remain steadfast. Because, the bottom may well fall out (John 16:33).

James does not remind his reader about Job to encourage more patience when trouble comes. Honestly, Job is neither patient nor without complaint. What he does is endure to the end. He suffers through his trials without throwing in the towel and cursing God. That's the real quality James illuminates.[130] Will we be faithful when the bottom falls out? Are we going to be women of faith, believing God is a God of mercy and goodness even when we cannot see how it's going to turn out? This is the mark of invincibility.

It's what we find happening in the life of Charles Spurgeon near the beginning of his ministry. Honestly, this one event should have been the end of him. When all should have been lost, it wasn't.

On October 19, 1856, Spurgeon and his ministry team rented Surrey Music Hall to accommodate the growing numbers coming to hear him preach. The balconies were filled, the room at capacity, holding roughly twelve thousand people. As the first service began, someone yelled, "Fire! The galleries are giving away, the place is falling!" Panic struck across the building, causing a stampede toward the exits. In the uproar and hysteria, seven people died and several others were seriously injured.[131] There was no fire. It was all a hoax out of jealousy and meanness.

Spurgeon had to be carried off the stage and could not even stand the sight of his Bible for weeks. He did return to the congregants he would pastor over the next thirty years. In speaking of the faithfulness of God in despair, he said these words:

I have gone to the very bottoms of the mountains, as some of you know, in a night that never can be erased from my memory, a night connected with this place. And I have had to pass through severe personal bodily pain. But as far as my witness goes, I can say that he is able to save unto the uttermost and in the last extremity, and he has been a good God to me.[132]

BECOMING INVINCIBLE—

Beth Moore reminds us that faith is not believing in our own unshakable belief, but in believing in an unshakable God.[133] My encouragement to you is to read dead people, like Elizabeth Elliot, Amy Carmichael and Corrie Ten Boom who knew God's unshakable quality and demonstrated it through their lives. Read about dead people like Rosa Parks, Evangeline Cory Booth and Charlotte "Lottie" Moon. Get to know alive people who have a little or a lot of gray hair and some stories to tell of God's faithfulness. Adding this to your Bible reading will help inspire your legs with what they need to stand immovable, even when the earth gives way.

Day 75:
Failing Forward Feat #8

You have to be a new person, you can't just make new
decisions.

~John Piper[134]

One Sunday morning, Shawn Turner and his son were driving
along the Boca Raton canal when they noticed a car floating in
the water. Bystanders watched from the shore, taking photos. Turner
caught a glimpse of a passenger in the floating car and turned his
steering wheel in that direction. Within seconds of coming to a stop,
he was out of the truck and in the water, moving toward the scene.

After lowering the window, Turner dove head first into the
sinking car to free the unconscious driver. Without warning, the
SUV shifted, taking a sharp dive downward. Spectators urged him
to get out. Instead, Turner continued his rescue attempt. Moments
later, the man appeared with the previously trapped woman now
free in his arms, heading toward the shore, seconds before the canal
engulfed the vehicle. When asked why he did what he did, Turner
said, "Somebody had to act."[135]

This journey has largely been for you. How do you leave the
unseen, unimportant, insignificant you to embrace the regenerated,
known, loved, purpose-filled woman learning to become invincible
in Christ? Answering this question is how you and I become truly
seen, like a city on a hill, or a zebra in the middle of a herd of cows.
You will not be missed.

Important to grasp is that your new found identity is not just
about you. Sometimes people get off track. We drive headlong into

rushing rivers. Other times the movement away from Truth becomes so subtle we don't realize it until it's too late.

Our sojourning trailblazer for what it looks like to be the light in your dark environment, to Go and Show who God is and what He can do, knows firsthand, what it's like to be sinking unaware. So, his last word is tender, and turns us outward.

My brothers, if anyone among you wanders from the truth and someone brings him back, let him know that whoever brings back a sinner from his wandering will save his soul from death and will cover a multitude of sins.

James 5:19-20 ESV

James encourages us to *do something*. Don't just take a picture and watch the tragedy unfold. In his final words, he nudges us to take what we know and assume responsibility to help and restore one another.[136] People wander. Sin wins out in overrunning truth and turning hearts away from the Living God. Still, the hope oozing from the Bible remains in you, and in me, to do what we now know to do.

Shawn Turner is a plumber. He's not a member of Special Forces or a fireman. He likes to fish and surf. But when someone is in trouble and their life is on the line, he is a man of action. You and I should do likewise. The Word of God makes the dire situation clear. People's lives are at stake. You can be a part of turning a person drowning in sin back. It will save their very soul and they will be forgiven.

You, my friend, are needed. Take all you know with all you are still learning. Don't worry about your half-covered mud-clad fence. Just go help bring someone back to Jesus.

He is no fool who gives what he cannot keep, to gain what he cannot lose.

~Jim Elliot[137]

234

BECOMING INVINCIBLE—

Ask God to make you aware. Ask Him to give insight for how to approach those He would have you help. Do not watch from the sidelines. There is no settling for spectator Christianity for you. Plead for His courage to cover you in your effort. Then do what you never believed you could. Go. Go in your God-given spiritual invincibility. Move out in His strength, trusting God will have gone before you, softening that person's heart to lead them back to Himself. Then thank the Lord for transforming you, enabling a wallflower nobody to participate in someone's eternity.

AFTERWORD

LACKING IN NOTHING

The LORD will perfect that which concerns me; Your mercy,
O LORD, endures forever; Do not forsake the works of Your
hands.

Psalm 138:8 NKJV

I found myself driving down a lonely Texas highway in my wall-flower wilderness, pondering my state of affairs. Alone in the car, I did what you might do. I prayed out loud, "Lord, what's wrong with me?" Less than two miles later, I encountered that field of cows with a zebra in the center for the first time.

That visual changed my life. Sometimes God does that. He gives a phrase, an incident, a paragraph, slogan, song, or image as you are driving along that sticks. That's what I am hoping I have done for you. It's what I pray some of the stories shared will do and the mark our focus on James leaves. I pray God uses these to help the principles get you out of the shadows, moving you further down the road so that you become perfect and complete in your faith, lacking in nothing.

Before we turn the final page and you embark upon the next steps in your journey, allow me to share one more example. One more herd member turned zebra. Another whose light shone before those around him, right where God planted him, in striking brilliance for the Kingdom.

237

Cross the ocean with me in a sail-powered ship to London in the year 1780. That's the year William Wilberforce won his seat in the House of Commons. At twenty-one, Wilberforce began a fifty-year investment in the political life of England. And we are ever grateful.

His first years as a politician were largely spent with the herd. He was a wealthy, smooth-talking bachelor without a care in the world. When Congress was not in session, he spent his holidays traveling with family and friends. On one of these breaks, a friend named Isaac Milner led him intellectually to Christianity. It wasn't until later Wilberforce understood the full force of grace and forgiveness, or what he called "the great change." But when he did, the man was never the same.

Wilberforce felt he had squandered his opportunities and best years of his life on nothingness. Wasted years, never to be recovered. Unsure if political life (or remaining with his herd) was the right path, he sought out John Newton (pastor and author of "Amazing Grace"), who offered timely advice and encouragement. In a letter to a searching Wilberforce, he wrote among other encouragements, "It is hoped and believed that the Lord has raised you up for the good of His church and for the good of the nation."[138]

William was encouraged to do just that. He stayed in the herd. But for the next eleven years, every free moment, instead of squandering the time on vain pursuits, he studied the Bible. Nine or ten hours a day, he examined the Scriptures when not in session. The rest of the time he spent alone in prayer, as if to make up for lost time. By 1787, he felt he had direction or a calling from God in the space God marked out for him. Wilberforce came to understand his task was to bring about the abolition of the slave trade and slavery altogether in England. In May of 1789, he spoke publicly to the House of Commons, declaring come what may, he would never rest until he could help bring about that very thing.[139]

Wilberforce spent the next twenty years working toward that aim. He did not fit in. There was much opposition including death threats, physical maladies, family problems, myriad failings, disappointments, and loss. Yet, he did not quit, even when he felt alone or was alone. The man who was once comfortable living his ordinary life, fitting in with his homies, fought until his dying breath on behalf of those who had no voice, so that three days before his death, the abolition of slavery was signed into law by an overwhelming majority, even with cheers ringing out. It only took the rest of his life.

How does one person impact those around him like this man? If you were to make a closer examination, you would discover he simply learned how to Go and Show like we are. He did it until Jesus took him home.

The reason I share his journey with you, and those of others along the same path, is because of our deep neediness. I can read the statistics. There isn't a girl, young adult, or middle-aged woman I encounter to whom this message does not resonate to some degree. We are people who need help in the emotionally trying places. Our capacities for surviving and thriving in the face of criticism and opposition are not naturally high.[140] On our own, we navigate quickly back to the corner, hidden and overlooked, when God made us for something entirely different.

Make no mistake, there will be opposition. People will not like you at times, no matter how hard you try, or how brightly you shine. You might pick up your phone one day, just to listen to a twenty-minute rant from someone you thought was your friend declaring, "Every word that comes out of your mouth is hateful." (She could give no examples, but vehemently stood by her claim.)

Go ahead. Cry. That's what I did. But recognize assessments like these are not genuine realities. So press on, my friend, toward what you know to be true. Yes, you and I might need more mud on our fences, but the Lord will not forsake the work of His hands. Thank God we are in progress—more black-and-white-striped than we once appeared. When perfect and complete come together, the result is a person fulfilling what God approves and requires for her life.[141]

What if your pain-filled wallflower days were to prepare you for becoming the zebra? Hold on to the reminder, the word, the example, or the vision that helps you know how dear you are to your Father and how deeply He wants to fulfill in you and through you a work of His glorious design. May the Lord show Himself faithful in your Going and Showing all the days of your life.

This is what the LORD says:

I will answer you in a time of favor,

and I will help you in the day of salvation.

I will keep you, and I will appoint you

to be a covenant for the people,

to restore the land,

to make them possess the desolate inheritances,

Saying to the prisoners, "Come out,"

and to those who are in darkness, "Show yourselves."

Isaiah 49:8-9 CSB

This is my story. It is a story of an invisible girl made invincible by the One who sees me, who hears me, who knows me, and loves me more than I can comprehend. My prayer for you is that you allow the Word of God to speak to you through my wallflower story and the wealth of biblical examples provided so that you experience true and lasting transformation. I have no doubt I am no longer hidden. You can see me now. The question remains, will we see you?

My Personal Plan for Becoming Invincible

Leave the broken, irreversible past in God's hands, and step
out into the invincible future with Him.

~Oswald Chambers[142]

Part I: Saying Goodbye to My Wallflower Ways

(**Day 7**) What are the three major factors in your life that cause
you to feel alone, left out, or like a wallflower?

1. _____

_____

2. _____

_____

3. _____

_____

What do you believe keeps you in this perpetual wallflower mode?

_____

_____

(Day 12) Which, if any of these beliefs, have you tucked away in your _bucket of badness,_ to carry around year after year, from one season to the next? Check all that apply.

- o   God loves me like He loves everyone else—generally, not specifically.

- o   If I were only better, God would use me, too.

- o   If I were more like her, then God would listen to me.

- o   God doesn't answer my prayers because I'm not one of His favorites.

- o   God could never use me after what I've done.

- o   God doesn't want to help me.

- o   I am not worth listening to.

- o   God is not my problem, people are my problem.

- o   God does not want to bless me.

- o   God is just about done with me.

What truths have you uncovered so far in this journey forward that will help unload your baggage and replace that wrong theology?

_____

_____

_____

_____

What questions remain?

_____

_____

_____

_____

First of all, you want to seek out if these are questions the Bible can answer for itself. Sometimes, I can Google my question and follow the leads to a trustworthy Bible-based site to see how the Bible answers my question about the Bible. There is nothing wrong with seeking out answers to difficult questions. Secondly, you and I should pray. Pray for God to bring clarity or help. And if these don't suffice, get wise counsel. Seek out a friend, mentor, or pastor. Finally, you will need to decide what to do with the answers received.

You might not like or agree with the answers you get. But you liking them doesn't make the answers any less true or any more false. In our early married life, my husband, Chad—whose training was scientific and intellectual—didn't see the Bible that way. (Some steeped in theological training don't either.) His was a mixture of all three.

About two or three years after I made my purchase of the One Year Bible, we moved into a Sunday School class taught by Dr. Glen Brindley. Dr. Brindley was an ophthalmologist with a background in zoology from a state university. But this man believed the Bible is the very Word of God. Every week he taught the Bible as the Words of God—all of them—and explained that the believer cannot pick and choose the ones he likes and reject the ones he doesn't. Believing the Bible is not like eating in a cafeteria. You take it all or leave it all.

Chad brought questions every week that all began the same way. "Dr. Brindley, are you saying that you believe …" Dr. Brindley would smile, nodding in agreement that yes, he did, indeed, believe what the Bible said about whatever Chad called into question this time. They would talk a bit about the particulars of why and how. But in the end, it was a choice for Chad to make. In time, he decided to take it all. Like my life-changing decision to purchase that One Year Bible, this one choice made the same lasting difference in him.

The Bible is not like a smorgasbord you find in a cafeteria. A Christian takes it all, believing it with her mind, heart and life, or she leaves it all. You will need to make that choice for yourself.

(Day 15) To move from wallflower mode to becoming visible, we need to remind ourselves of what is true. Regularly. Below is a small arsenal of verses. Put them on your phone. Jot them on notecards. Write them on sticky notes. Memorize them if it helps. But know this: Every time something happens in your life that communicates you are worthless, or those familiar sensations of loneliness, isolation, and forgottenness settle over you like storm clouds in hurricane season, use the Truth of God's Word to pry you from the wallpaper.

☑ 1 John 3:1

☑ Ephesians 2:10

☑ 1 Peter 2:9

☑ Galatians 2:6

☑ Romans 5:20

☑ Psalm 37:40

☑ 1 Peter 3:12

☑ 1 Peter 5:8

☑ Ephesians 1:3

☑ Psalm 136:1

(Day 17) My chosen prayer time is:

_____

My chosen prayer spot is:

_____

What does the prospect of no longer being unseen mean to me?

_____

_____

_____

(Day 19) Jesus reminds us that every believer in Christ is to live like a city on a hill or a lamp lighting up a room. What does it look like to be light in your everyday life right now?

_____

_____

(Day 20) John the Baptist shows us one main truth:

Going and Showing is to

_____

_____

What would it look like for you to decrease and Him to increase in your daily routine?

_____

_____

In your relationships?

_____

_____

(Day 21) What about *your circumstance* would you like God to change?

_____

_____

What about *you* would you like God to change?

_____

_____

_____

_____

(Day 24) Where is God's strategic placement of you?

_____

_____

What is one specific way you can embrace the space God has given you?

_____

_____

(Day 26) Of all the privileges and benefits Paul articulates belonging to every believer in Christ in Ephesians 1:3-14, which one speaks the most to your needs today?

_____

_____

Which one is the most difficult to believe and receive as your own?

_____

_____

What is one truth from Part I that is most meaningful to you?

_____

_____

_____

_____

When we begin to understand how God relates to us, personally, we can start coming away from the sidelines and allow Him to liberate us from loneliness and that sense of being left behind.

Part II: Becoming Visible

(**Day 27**) When it comes to a calling or what God has for you and I to do, sometimes we simply don't know. We hang onto the railings at the outskirts of the room and blend into the curtains because we have no idea how we are spiritually qualified to do anything else.

Spiritual Gifts: The Bible assures us you and I have a spiritual gift (at least one) and the exercise of it is necessary for the health of the Body of Christ. Lifeway Christian Resources offers three free online tools to help you learn about spiritual gifts and discover how you are gifted to serve: including a Spiritual Gifts list, a Spiritual Gift survey, and a tool for honing in on where you feel God leading you to serve. You can access them from your computer or mobile device at no cost by going to Lifeway.com at https://www.lifeway.com/en/articles/women-leadership-spiritual-gifts-growth-service.

When you have an idea where your spiritual gifting lies, write what you learn below.

_____

_____

Begin praying how God would have you utilize your gifts for His Kingdom where you are. Look for opportunities at your church. Pray for God's leadership. This is mainly where He grows and develops us. Don't be afraid to try something outside your wheelhouse.

Personality Assessment: Another avenue to help navigate a way forward, away from the sidelines is to learn about your personality type. There are many resources available that help determine strengths along with weaknesses. Myers-Briggs is a well-known assessment that has been used for many years. You can access a free version on-line here: http://www.humanmetrics.com/personality. If you choose to try one, record the results below.

_____

_____

(Day 28) Pray: Psalm 90:16-17 "Let your work be shown to your servants, and your glorious power to their children" (ESV). Write these and other verses that deal with your purpose on notecards you can begin taking into your prayer times. Or use a prayer app, like Echo (free version). Keep a prayer journal and fill it with Scripture you can pray.

All of these efforts will help equip you for better serving in the way God has gifted you. But James still has it right. Whether your place is in the front where everyone knows you or behind closed doors when no one sees you are there, our identity remains the same. I am Cheri Strange, a servant of God and of Jesus Christ. Who are you?

_____

_____

(Day 29) Identify your tribe: Do you have your people in the correct circles? Ask the Lord to orchestrate and build your relationships.

Bulls-Eye: 2-5 people

_____

_____

_____

_____

First Circle: About 15 people (co-workers, relatives, friends—people important to you)

_____

_____

_____

_____

Second Circle: About 50 people (acquaintances) (Recognize, we sometimes get people in the wrong circles.)

_____

_____

_____

_____

_____

_____

(Day 30) Give yourself permission not to participate in the relationship drama unfolding around you. Think about it now. What can you do when you find yourself in the midst of some drama you did not create? Remain silent? Stay calm and cordial? Ignore the attacker? Keep drinking your lemonade?

_____

_____

_____

_____

(Day 31) When it comes to fighting for your joy, take three action steps:

1) Pray for it

2) Be thankful

3) Remind yourself of God's track record

(Day 34) James, Paul, and even Jesus declare that when God forgives a person and the Holy Spirit enters a person's life, there will be evidence. What evidence is there in your life that you have been transformed by the power of the Holy Spirit?

_____

_____

_____

_____

(Day 35) Recognize in your plan to become the most visible and vibrant version of yourself, God may see fit to leave your situation unchanged. Without the desired miracle. Is there any situation in which God is requiring you to be content in your weakness so that His strength may be seen through your life? If so, describe it here.

_____

_____

_____

_____

(Day 36) How to Fight for Joy: Review the action steps we discussed and commit them to memory for when you need them.

- o   Call on God for help

- o   Move your eyes off your problems

- o   Focus on _____

- o   Hold onto Praise and _____

(Day 39) Are you prone to draw near to God, or do you need to work toward coming in closer? What is a next step you can take to move closer than you are today?

_____

_____

_____

_____

(Day 43) John Owen writes, "Be killing sin, or sin will be killing you."[143] You and God know your struggles with sin. Everyone has them. Make a 3-step plan of action for how you will "be killing sin" in your own life for the next 60 days.

1. _____

_____

2. _____

_____

3. _____

_____

(Day 45) Identify your three triggers for sending you back to the corner. (Be sure to complete the activity for the day, dealing with your social accounts.)

_____

_____

(Day 46) Listen Well: What Bible will you listen to over the next few months:

_____

_____

Where and when will you listen:

_____

_____

Which podcasts are you going to follow this season?

_____

_____

How often will you attend church; and what will you do to become a better listener?

_____

_____

Part III: Making Room in my life to be seen

(Day 47) When you feel like you cannot hear God, or like maybe what you thought you heard was really something you made up in your head, take these three action steps:

☑ Remember, you are not alone

☑ Continue the conversation

☑ Look to God's Word for His response

(Day 51) What verse or verses most help to remind you of your limitlessness in Christ?

_____

_____

(Day 52) What two ways can you take more control over your mouth?

_____

_____

(Day 53) Ask God to reveal any attitudes you currently hold that show favoritism toward someone, or a group whether it be for economic, racial, educational, or political differences or something else. A zebra in the making shows no partiality, but understands the Gospel truth of Colossians 3:11 and James 2:1-9. Ask God to reveal any and all attitudes you hold that run contrary to His Word, and to help you be a defender of justice when needed regardless of the cost.

_____

(Day 54) In what way, if any, would you say you are a friend of the world?

_____

_____

Write your prayer asking for grace, believing it will be given.

_____

_____

(Day 55) Are you a judgmental person? Overly critical? Quick to find fault? Are you energized to spill the tea or tell the gossip you know about someone? James calls us back to what we learned in our childhoods. You need a strategy for dealing with any attitudes of your own that may surface. The first step should be to ask the Lord for forgiveness.

What will be your next step?

_____

_____

(Day 56) I mentioned I wore a bracelet with the words "Believe God" engraved on it for about thirteen years. I wore it until I didn't need the physical reminder on my wrist anymore. If you need something tangible like that, here is a link for instructions to make one yourself.

Check out https://www.countrypeony.com/blog/diy-colorful-alphabet-bracelet. If you would prefer buying one, visit https://store.sheyearns.com/collections/jewelry.

Part IV: Becoming Vibrant

(Day 58) What desert places has God brought you out from?

_____

_____

Where is He leading you?

_____

_____

(Day 59) What thoughts are you prone to listen to that pull you away from the Truth God declares about you?

_____

_____

What is one step you can take to stop listening to those destructive lies and receive the _implanted Word?_

_____

_____

(Day 60) I died a slow death to what I thought I needed to be seen. You can side-step all my detours and heartache by looking to Jesus to be your audience. Care what He alone thinks. Ask Him to help you establish Him as your audience of One, making everyone else irrelevant.

_____

_____

(Day 62) Find time to keep your eyes peeled and your ears attentive to needs. What can you do? Note, you will need to make time for it. This afternoon, I am driving an hour one way to meet someone because she needs a friend. I can just tell. It doesn't matter that I don't have the time. And she doesn't need to know. I will simply show up for her. What will the Lord have you do?

_____

_____

(Day 63) Has the Lord burdened you with a desire to meet a greater need? An injustice, or help in a cause? Pray about the problem. Ask God to bring solutions. If you are to be part of the solution, what would he have you do?

_____

_____

(Day 65) List three behaviors or attitudes you need to adopt as an heir of the Kingdom and a child of the King.

1. _____

_____

2. _____

_____

3. _____

_____

Part V: Becoming Spiritually Invincible

(**Day 66**) What do you feel should be your next step as we come to the final pages of this journey together?

_____

_____

_____

_____

(**Day 67**) Often, an act of spiritual invincibility looks like doing the only thing you know to do. Stepping out, taking a risk because you believe God has asked you to do so. Take a moment to pray, asking God to give you this courage and an obedience to follow when the nudging comes.

_____

_____

(**Day 72**) What do you feel God is dreaming for your life?

_____

_____

(**Day 73**) What two actions can you take the next time you find yourself waiting?

1. _____

_____

2. _____

_____

(Day 75) Is there anyone you know who needs encouragement or the loving arm of Truth in the way James describes to help bring them back to Jesus?

_____

_____

The fact that it's here communicates our need to be mindful and keep our eyes and hearts open. Lives depend upon it, and God means to use you.

If you have made it to this final step, what has happened in my life over the last years, I pray is happening or will happen to you. God's power, presence, and work in my life brought me courage, strength, and a freedom to stand where I never felt welcome, equipped, or worthy. He did it, and I could no longer keep the reality to myself. This song has been stuck in my head and heart since it came out. Find "How Could I Be Silent" by Caitie Hurst wherever you get your music. Play it on repeat. Make it your testimonial mantra as well. I hope you love her as much as I do.

My encouragement is for you to keep working your plan. Sling that mud. Keep failing forward. Even if your circumstances do not change, you, my friend, can. Put what you have learned into practice. Trust that God can do in and through you more than you can ask or imagine. Pray the prayers, utilize the Scripture, and put into motion the action steps you have laid out on the pages.

But what should you do next? Where should you pick up? How do you distinguish the important from the urgent? What does it look like in your everyday life to Go and Show while you are ever in process?

Do the next thing. Begin in the place God gives you the inkling to start. Can you do all you want at once? No. Will it happen as fast as you desire? Probably not. Just do the next thing God shows you to do, and leave everything else to Him.

As you go, allow me to send you out with a prayer.

Lord, I thank you for being the unrelenting seeker of the one the world deems insignificant and the one who feels forgotten and invisible. You know every hurt, disappointment, and failure, as well the triumphs and successes. Use your Word to help her know your Truth about how You see her and how You want her to live out her life. Give her sweet relationships with those who recognize her worth and beauty. But also give her courage to stand alone in a crowd, mixed with a fearlessness showing who You are in the day-to-day duties of life. Equip her for every good work you have already prepared for her to do. But above all, in her quest to be seen, make her unseen, shadowed only by the likeness of Your Son shining through her.

In the Name of Jesus, Amen.

LETTER TO THE READER

Dear fellow zebra in the making,

What did you think of *CAN YOU SEE ME, NOW?* I know you could have picked any number of books to read, but you picked this book, and for that I am grateful. I pray it equipped you with hope, direction, and value for your everyday life. If it has made an impact, it would be great if you could share this book with friends and family by posting it on Facebook, Instagram, and Twitter.

If you enjoyed this book and found some benefit in reading it, I'd love to hear from you. Jot me a note at info@sheyearns.com. And I hope you could take a moment to post a review on Amazon. Your feedback is very important. The support will help get the message into more hands that need it; and it helps me, as the author, improve my skills in communicating for future projects.

Many prayers have been prayed for you. Thank you for being here. I am ever grateful to walk this journey with you.

For His Glory,

Cheri

ACKNOWLEDGMENTS

This girl would never have made it past the first rejection if God did not gift Chad Strange to me as my lifelong partner. Not only does he offer a timely word, he is wise and savvy, steering me ahead when I feel like running back to my comfortable corner. For his wisdom and tireless enthusiasm, I am eternally grateful.

Falling in close behind him are my children. From the grown and flown ones who listen like a good friend, to the constant sacrifices being made by the ones at home to "let Mom write," I am thankful beyond words. A house filled with people is not the most ideal place to create, but you made quiet space for the needs.

For Karen and George Porter of Bold Vision Books, I am indebted. Karen is responsible for teaching me the publishing ropes from the beginning and has been a mentor to me before I knew I needed one. Rhonda Rhea offers great insight I need with much enthusiasm. Kaley Rhea, who edited the project, brings a keen eye. This team is a winning one, and I am grateful to be a part of what God is doing through them.

To my prayer warriors, Carolyn Merrill, Heather Dupont, Holly Mayes, Fran Strange, Kimberly Ross, Margey Watson, Stephanie Cartwright, and Esther Smith, I am indebted. Thank you for your support in prayer and your listening ears through this project. And to the women of She Prays, I thank you for doing what you do so well.

A special thank you belongs to Katie Reid, who showed up in my life at just the right time with the wisdom, encouragement, and ideas to help make this project a reality. And when it became such Karen Sargent, Stacey Thacker, and Rob Eager were there to help get the message out in a way you needed it. For each one God brought into view to help make this book available, I am eternally grateful.

Meet Cheri Strange

Cheri Strange is living proof of God's ability to transform a plain and ordinary wallflower into something completely unexpected. She did not set out to become a writer or a speaker, nor did she dream of getting a Ph.D. and becoming the mother to eight children. She simply fell in love with a God who met her where she lived—in the shadows. When she began to hear His call to move beyond the sidelines and away from the wall, she responded.

Today, she communicates the truths of this magnificent Savior plainly for others to know as well. Her writing and speaking ministry, She Yearns Ministries, is all about encouraging women to desire more of God in their everyday lives. She is a YouVersion Partner, providing devotional content across the globe, and the author of the Bible study, *Life Principles for Living Out the Greatest Commandment*.

Dr. Strange holds a Ph.D. from Baylor University in Educational Psychology and a Master's degree from Hardin Simmons University. Cheri and her husband, Chad, are raising six girls and twin boys. You can find her at SheYearns.com, on the YouVersion app, or hunting for the best tortilla soup in Houston.

Bible Version Permissions

Endnotes

INTRODUCTION
1   Cheyenne, "Popular," Whisper, accessed September 26, 2020, http://whisper.sh/w/MzU1Mjg5NzY3.

2   Cigna, Loneliness Index Report: Survey of 20,000 Americans Examining Behaviors Driving Loneliness in the United States, (Bloomfield: Cigna, 2018), https://www.cigna.com/static/www-cigna-com/docs/about-us/newsroom/studies-and-reports/combatting-loneliness/loneliness-survey-2018-full-report.pdf.

CHAPTER 1
3   2020. Dictionary.com. Accessed 09 26, 2020. https://www.dictionary.com/browse/wallflower.

4   Herbert C. Woolston and George F. Root, *Jesus Loves the Little Children*, http://www.hymntime.com/tch/htm/j/e/s/l/jesloves.htm, accessed 10 20, 2021.

5   Kimberly Holland, "Childhood Emotional Neglect: How it Can Impact You Now and Later," Healthline, accessed October 21, 2021, https://www.healthline.com/health/mental-health/childhood-emotional-neglect.

6   Kari A. Gleiser, "Seeing the Invisible: The Role of Recognition in Healing from Neglect and Deprivation," AEDP Institute, last updated January 15, 2022, https://aedpinstitute.org/wp-content/uploads/page_Seeing-the-Invisible.pdf.

7   Cigna, Loneliness Index Report.

8   "The Christmas Cookie Club Quotes by Ann Pearlman," Goodreads, accessed November 18, 2021, https://www.goodreads.com/work/quotes/6750795-the-christmas-cookie-club.

9   C.S. Lewis, *Mere Christianity* (1952; Harper Collins: 2001) 215-216.

10   Charles H. Spurgeon, "Charles Spurgeon Quotes," O Christian, accessed October 10, 2021, http://christian-quotes.ochristian.com/Charles-Spurgeon-Quotes/page-5.shtml.

11   Harvey Mackay, "Charles Shultz Learned from Rejection--So Can You," *Star Tribune*, August 05, 2018, www.startribune.com/mackay-charles-schulz-learned-from-rejection-so-can-you/490028951.

12   Matt Weinberger, "This is Why Steve Jobs Got Fired from Apple--and How He Came Back to Save the Company," *Business Insider*, July 13, 2017, www.businessinsider.com/steve-jobs-apple-fired-returned-2017-7.

13   Nadia Goodman, "Dyson on Using Failure to Drive Success" *Entrepreneur*, November 05, 2012, www.entrepreneur.com/article/224855.

14   "Sir James Dyson net worth: Sunday Times Rich List 2021," *The Sunday Times*, accessed April 2, 2022, https://www.thetimes.co.uk/article/sunday-times-rich-list-sir-james-dyson-singapore-brexit-wealth-wfkqccw97.

15   Aiden Wilson Tozer, "Aiden Wilson Quotes," Brainy Quote, accessed November 17, 2021, https://www.brainyquote.com/quotes/aiden_wilson_tozer_153969.

16   Elizabeth Elliot, "Elizabeth Elliot Quotes," Good Reads, accessed April 3, 2022, https://www.goodreads.com/author/quotes/6264.Elisabeth_Elliot.

17   Babbie Mason, "About Babbie Mason," Babbie Mason, accessed April 14, 2022, https://babbie.com/babbie-mason.

Chapter 2
18   Jeff Kinney, "Middle School Quotes," Wise Sayings, accessed May 26, 2021, www.wisesayings.com/middle-school-quotes/#ixzz6vyK11jkm.

19   Thomas Whitelaw, *The Pulpit Commentary*, edited by H.E.M. Spence and Joseph Exell, vol. 1, Genesis (Grand Rapids, Michigan: Wm. B. Eerdmans Publishing Company, 1950).

20   Ralph Waldo Emerson, "Ralph Waldo Emerson Quotes," Quotations Page, accessed May 05, 2021, http://www.quotationspage.com/quotes/Ralph_Waldo_Emerson/.

21   Oprah Winfrey, "Oprah Winfrey Quotes," Good Reads, accessed September 05, 2020, https://www.goodreads.com/quotes/392086-can-you-see-me-can-you-hear-me-does-anything.

22   Gloria Vanderbilt, "Gloria Vanderbilt Quotes," Brainy Quote, accessed May 26, 2021, http://www.brainyquote.com/quotes/gloria_vanderbilt_530067.

23   R.C. Sproul, *Essential Truths of the Christian Faith Illustrated* (Carolstream, Illinois: Tyndale House, 1998).

24   Unknown. *He's Got the Whole World in His Hands*, Stephen Griffith, accessed October 10, 2021, http://www.stephengriffith.com/folksongindex/hes-got-the-whole-world-in-his-hands/.

25   House to House Heart to Heart, "Why Did the Jews and Samaritans Hate Each Other So Much," House to House Heart to Heart, accessed April 14, 2022, https://housetohouse.com/jews-samaritans-hate-one-another-much/.

26   Elizabeth Elliot, "15 Christian Quotes by Amazing Godly Women," Christian Quotes, accessed April 3 2022, https://www.christianquotes.info/top-quotes/15-christian-quotes-by-amazing-godly-women/.

27   Anne Graham Lotz, "Anne Graham Lotz Quotes," Brainy Quote, accessed April 14, 2022, https://www.brainyquote.com/authors/anne-graham-lotz-quotes.

Chapter 3
28   C.S. Lewis, *The Silver Chair* (New York, New York: Harper Collins, 2009).

29   Adi Guarjardo, "Are Zebras Legal in Texas?" *KENS5 CBS*, August 9, 2019, https://www.kens5.com/article/life/are-zebras-legal-in-texas/273-a8b99f24-eb02-4779-a790-f65d4d72624b.

30   Josh Baldwin, et al, "Stand in Your Love," Bethel Music, 2018.

31   C.S. Lewis, "C. S. Lewis Quotes," Brainy Quote, accessed May 26, 2021, www.brainyquote.com/quotes/c_s_lewis_714968.

32   Timothy Keller, *Preaching: Communicating Faith in an Age of Skepticism* (Westminster, London: Penguin Books, 2015).

33   Stephen Miller, "What Happened to Jesus' Brothers? The Post Gospel Life of the Disciples," *Christianity Today* Issue 59 (1998): www.christianitytoday.com/history/issues/issue-59/what-happened-to-jesus-brother.html.

34   Eusebius Pamphilius, "Eusebius: The Martyrdom of James, who was Called the Brother of the Lord," Preterist Archive, accessed September 25, 2020, https://web.archive.org/web/20190421191937/https://www.preteristarchive.com/0325_eusebius_the-martyrdom-of-james-who-was-called-the-brother-of-the-lord/.

35   Robert D. Richardson, "Henry Thoreau: A Life of the Mind," Walden, accessed May 26, 2021, https://www.walden.org/what-we-do/library/thoreau/mis-quotations/.

36   Khameeka Kitt, "Other Fun Stuff," Stanford at the Tech Understand Genetics, August 31, 2011, http://genetics.thetech.org/ask/ask426.

37   Cristen Conger, "Are Zebras Black wih White Stripes or White with Black Stripes?" How Stuff Works, accessed July 26, 2021, https://animals.howstuffworks.com/mammals/zebra-stripes1.htm.

38   Priscilla Shirer, "Priscilla Shirer Quotes," AZ Quotes, accessed April 3, 2022, https://www.azquotes.com/author/46257-Priscilla_Shirer.

39   Ray VanderLaan, "Gezer," That the World May Know, accessed September 05, 2020, https://www.thattheworldmayknow.com/gezer.

40   John Piper, "John Piper Quotes," Brainy Quotes, accessed May 26, 2021, www.brainyquotes.com/quotes/john_piper_605831.

41   Crossway, "Echoes of Jesus Sermon on the Mount in James," accessed September 06, 2020, https://www.esv.org/resources/esv-global-study-bible/chart/59-01/.

42   Joyce Meyer, *Approval Addiction: Overcoming Your Need to Please Everyone* (Brentwood, Tennessee: FaithWorks, 2005).

CHAPTER 4
43   Martin Luther King, Jr, "Martin Luther King, Jr. Quotes," AZ Quotes, accessed November 16, 2021, https://www.azquotes.com/quote/444941?ref=servant-of-god.

44   Louie Giglio, "Louie Giglio Quotes," AZ Quotes, accessed November 16, 2021, https://www.azquotes.com/author/22501-Louie_Giglio?p=2.

45   Craig Groeschel, "Craig Groeschel Quotes," AZ Quotes, accessed November 16, 2021, https://www.azquotes.com/author/18505-Craig_Groeschel.

46   Zoya Gervis, 2019. "Average American has This Many Actual Friends, Study Determines," Fox News Channel, May 11, 2019, https://www.foxnews.com/lifestyle/american-number-actual-friends-study-determines.

47   Tim Smedley, "Dunbar's Number: Why We Can Only Maintain 150 Relationships," BBC, accessed July 12, 2021, https://www.bbc.com/future/article/20191001-dunbars-number-why-we-can-only-maintain-150-relationships.

48   Smedley, "Dunbar's Numbers."

49   Anne Graham Lotz, *Jesus in Me: Experiencing the Holy Spirit as a Constant Companion* (Colorado Springs, Colorado: Multnoma, 2019).

50   Aurelius Augustine, *Confessions*, edited by Trans. R.S. Pine-Coffin (New York, New York: Penguin, 2019).

51   David Mathis, "In and Out, In a Blaise of Glory," Desiring God, accessed October 20, 2021, https://www.desiringgod.org/articles/in-and-out-in-a-blaise-of-glory.

52   Warren W. Wiersbe, *Bible Expository Commentary*, Logos Bible Software (Wheaton, Illinois: Victory Books, 2019).

53   Meyer, *Approval Addiction.*

54   "Penny Drop Myth," Mythbusters Fandom, accessed October 20, 2020, https://mythbusters.fandom.com/wiki/Penny_Drop_Myth.

55   "Do You Have to Wait 30 Minutes After Eating Before Swimming?" *UMASHealth*, 201, accessed October 20, 2021, https://uamshealth.com/medical-myths/do-you-have-to-wait-30-minutes-after-eating-before-swimming/#:~:text=If%20you%20are%20swimming%20for,your%20stomach%20to%20pass%20through.

56   Tom Stafford, "How Liars Create the 'Illusion of Truth,'" BBC, accessed October 10, 2021, https://www.bbc.com/future/article/20161026-how-liars-create-the-illusion-of-truth.

57   Nikita Sagar, "85 Mother Teresa Quotes That Will Make You More Generous," My Droll, February 24, 2021, https://mydroll.com/85-mother-teresa-quotes-that-will-make-you-more-generous/.

58   Melissa H. Schmitt, Keenan Stears, Adrian M. Shrader, "Zebra Reduce Predation Risk in Mixed-Species Herds by Eavesdropping on Cues from Giraffe," *Behavioral Ecology* 27 (4): 1073–1077, DOI 10.1093/beheco/arw015.

59   Charles H. Spurgeon, "Marks of Faith," *Spurgeon Sermons*, vol. 7 (London: Funk and Wagnalls Company, 1900).

60   Martin Luther, "Martin Luther Quotes," Christian Quotes, accessed November 16, 2021, https://www.christianquotes.info/search/contentment.

61   John Piper, *When I Don't Desire God: How to Fight for Joy* (Wheaton, Illinois: Crossway Books, 2004).

CHAPTER 5
62   Sandra Grauschaupf, "Are Publishers Clearing House Sweepstakes Scams?" The Balance Every Day, accessed July 14, 2021. https://www.thebalanceeveryday.com/are-publishers-clearing-house-sweepstakes-scams-886968.

63   C. Jerdan, *The Pulpit Commentary*, edited by H.D.M. Spence and Joseph S. Exell, vol. 21, Thessalonians, Timothy, Titus, Philemon, Hebrews, James, (Grand Rapids, Michigan: Wm. B. Eerdmans Publishing Company, 1950).

64   Charles H. Spurgeon, "Spurgeon Sermons: All Joy in All trials," The Spurgeon Center, accessed November 15, 2021, https://www.spurgeon.org/resource-library/sermons/all-joy-in-all-trials/#flipbook/.

65   J.A. MacDonald, *The Pulpit Commentary*, edited by H.D.M. Spence and Joseph S. Exell vol. 15, Matthew, 120 (Grand Rapids, Michigan: Wm. B. Eerdmans Publishing Company, 1950).

66   Cigna, Cigna Resilience Index: 2020 U. S. Report (Bloomfield, CT: Cisgna, 2020), https://cignaresilience.com/wp-content/uploads/2020/10/Cigna_ResilienceReport_FINAL.pdf.

67   Douglas J. Moo, *The Letter of James: An Introduction and Commentary* (Westmont, Illinois: Inter-Varsity Press, 1985).

68   CeCe Winans, "CeCe Winans Quotes," All Christian Quotes, accessed November 16, 2020, https://www.allchristianquotes.org/quotes/CeCe_Winans/6436.

69   Ronald J. Blue, "James," *The Bible Expository Commentary*. Logos Bible Software (Wheaton, Illinois: Victory Books, Inc., 1996).

70   Warren W. Wiersbe, *The Bible Expository Commentary*. Logos Bible Software (Wheaton, Illinois: Victory Books, Inc., 1996).

71   Alfred Lord Tennyson, "Locksley Hall," Poetry Foundation, accessed November 09, 2021. https://www.poetryfoundation.org/poems/45362/locksley-hall.

72   Craig Groeschel, *Weird: Because Normal Isn't Working* (Grand Rapids, Michigan: Zondervan, 2011).

CHAPTER 6
73   New World Encyclopedia contributors, "Zebra," *New World Encyclopedia*, accessed November 11, 2021, https://www.newworldencyclopedia.org/p/index.php?title=Zebra&oldid=1056259.

74   Rachel Wolchin, "The Good," The Good, accessed November 11, 2021, https://www.thegood.co/author/rachel-wolchin/.

75   Carrie Arnold, "The Difference Between Being a Victim and Having a Victim Mindset," blog, The Willow Group, April, 2018, https://www.willow-group.com/blog/the-difference-between-being-a-victim-and-having-a-victim-mindset.

76   William Barclay, *The Letters of James and Peter: The Daily Study Bible Series* (Philadelphia, Pennsylvania: The Westminster Press, 1976).

77   Amy Carmichael, *Edges of His Ways: Selections for Daily Reading* (Pennsylvania: CLC Publications, 1980).

78   Corrie Ten Boom, "Corrie Ten Boom Quotes," Good Reads, accessed November 16, 2021, https://www.goodreads.com/author/quotes/102203.Corrie_ten_Boom.

79   Peter H. Davids, *NIGTC: The Epistle of James, A Commentary of the Greek Text* (Grand Rapids: William B Eerdmans Publishing Company, 1982).

80   Tim Arango, "California Wildfires: Human Causes Arson," New York Times, August 20, 2018, https://www.nytimes.com/2018/08/20/us/california-wildfires-human-causes-arson.html.

81   John Wesley, "John Wesley Quotes," Good Reads, accessed 11 16, 2021, https://www.goodreads.com/quotes/576772-we-should-be-rigorous-in-judging-ourselves-and-gracious-in/.

82   Moo, *The Letter of James.*

83   Brennan Manning, *All is Grace: A Ragamuffin Memoir* (Colorado Springs, Colorado. David C. Cook, 2011).

84   Paulo Coelho, "Paulo Coelho Quotes," Quote Park, accessed November 02, 2021, https://quotepark.com/quotes/1043608-paulo-coelho-we-can-never-judge-the-lives-of-others-because-ea/.

85   Bonnie Allen, "American Becomes Foster Mom to 13," NPR, July 03, 2011, https://www.npr.org/2011/07/09/137348637/in-uganda-american-becomes-foster-mom-to-13-girls.

86   Hannah Whitall Smith, "Hannah Whitall Smith Quotes," AZ Quotes, accessed April 1, 2022, https://www.azquotes.com/author/21401-Hannah_Whitall_Smith.

87   Rosa Fox, "Looking Back the Day the Elephant Would not Cross the Bridge," *Finger Lakes Times*, September 03, 2020, https://www.fltimes.com/lifestyle/looking-back-the-day-the-elephant-would-not-cross-the-bridge/article_9d1e1b14-8e94-546e-8fdb-36f8d461e523.html.

Chapter 7
88   David Platt, *Radical: Taking Back Your Faith from the American Dream* (Colorado Springs, Colorado: Multnoma, 2010).

89   "Ponzi Scheme," Wikipedia, last modified March 18, 2022, https://en.wikipedia.org/wiki/Ponzi_scheme.

90   Warren W. Wiersbe, *50 People Every Christian Should Know: Learning from Spiritual Giants of the Faith* (Grand Rapids, Michigan: Baker Books, 2009).

91   Wiersbe, *50 People Every Christian.*

92   Wiersbe, *50 People Every Christian.*

93   Charles H. Spurgeon, "Brought Out to be Brought In," The Spurgeon Center for Biblical Preaching at Midwestern Seminary, accessed November 12, 2021, https://www.spurgeon.org/resource-library/sermons/brought-out-to-be-brought-in/#flipbook/.

94   John F. Walvoord, "John F. Walvoord Quotes," Christian Quotes, accessed November 16, 2021, https://www.christianquotes.info/quotes-by-topic/quotes-about-change/.

95   Harini Narayan, "Spreading Roots of the Strangler Ficus or Fig Tree," Harini Narayan, Accessed 10 15, 2021, https://mika-art.com/product/spreading-roots-of-the-strangler-ficus-or-fig-tree-yucatan/.

96   Alexander Maclaren, *Maclaren's Commentary: Expositions of Holy Scripture* (Harrington, Delaware: Delmarva Publications, Inc., 2013).

97   Maclaren, *Maclaren's Commentary.*

98   Dietrich Bonhoeffer, "Dietrich Bonhoeffer Quotes," A Z Quotes, accessed November 18, 2021, https://www.azquotes.com/quotes/topics/christian-fellowship.html.

99   Melissa Breyer, "10 Fascinating Facts About Zebras," Treehugger, accessed September 02, 2020, https://www.treehugger.com/things-you-didnt-know-about-zebras-4864185.

100   Ava James, "17 Friendship Quotes and 7 Steps to Being a Lifelong Friend," Praying with Confidence, October 17, 2020, https://praywithconfidence.com/christian-friendship-quotes/.

101   Jerdan, *The Pulpit Commentary.*

102   Jerdan, *The Pulpit Commentary.*

103   Peter Anderson, "Bible Verses About Faith: Uplifting Scripture to Give Hope in Hard Times," Bible Money Matters, last updated October 8, 2021, https://www.biblemoneymatters.com/bible-verses-about-faith/#:~:text=But%20someone%20will%20say%2C%20%E2%80%9CYou,I%20have%20kept%20the%20faith.&text=Ephesians%202%3A8%2D10%20For,have%20been%20saved%20through%20faith.

104   Clifton J. Allen, ed., The *Broadman Bible Commentary,* vol. 12 (Nashville, Tennessee: Broadman Press, 1972).

105   "Amy Carmichael," Wikipedia. last modified March 25, 2022, https://en.wikipedia.org/wiki/Amy_Carmichael.

106   Amy Carmichael, "Amy Carmichael Quotes," Quote Fancy, accessed November 11, 2021, https://quotefancy.com/amy-carmichael-quotes.

107   John Stott, "John Stott Quotes," Christian Quotes, accessed November 16, 2021, https://www.christianquotes.info/search/mercy.

108   MacClaren, *MacLaren's Commentary.*

109   Joyce Meyer, *Beauty for Ashes: Receiving Emotional Healing* (Franklin, Tennessee: FaithWords, 2008).

110   Rebecca J. Fowler, "Anastasia: The Mystery Resolved," *The Washington Post.* October 06, 1994, https://www.washingtonpost.com/archive/lifestyle/1994/10/06/anastasia-the-mystery-resolved/f208f264-a141-4f54-8354-934a3005f091/.

111   Fowler, "Anastasia: The Mystery Resolved."

CHAPTER 8
112   Fanny Crosby, "Give Me Jesus" Hymnary, accessed November 16, 2021, https://hymnary.org/hymn/CEL1997/554.
113   Allen, ed., *The Broadman Bible Commentary.*

114   Allen, ed., *The Broadman Bible Commentary.*

115   Charles H. Spurgeon, "The Arrows of the Bow Broken in Zion," The Spurgeon Center for Biblical Preaching at Midwestern Seminary, accessed September 25, 2021, https://www.ccel.org/ccel/spurgeon/sermons14/sermons14.iv.html.

116   John Piper, "John Piper Quotes," Brainy Quote, accessed November 16, 2021, https://www.brainyquote.com/quotes/john_piper_605818.

117   Kay Arthur, "Kay Arthur Quotes," Quote Fancy, accessed April 12, 2022, https://quotefancy.com/kay-arthur-quotes.

118   Stormie Omartain, "The Power of Praying Mom Quotes," Good Reads, accessed April 2, 2022, https://www.goodreads.com/work/quotes/16419428-the-power-of-a-praying-woman.

119   Dwight L. Moody, "Dwight L. Moody Quotes," Good Reads, accessed November 18, 2021, https://www.goodreads.com/author/quotes/5083573.Dwight_L_Moody.

120   Allen, ed., *The Broadman Bible Commentary*.

121   Matt Erickson, "Old Camel Knees: A brief Reflection on the Remarkable Prayer Life of James the Just,". *Renovate*, August 29, 2019, https://mwerickson.com/2019/08/29/old-camel-knees-a-brief-reflection-on-the-remarkable-prayer-life-of-james-the-just/.

122   Gift Guru Mona, "Gift Guru Mona Quotes," Good Reads, accessed April 2, 2022, https://www.goodreads.com/author/quotes/17555136.Gift_Gugu_Mona.

123   Charles H. Spurgeon, "The Story of God's Mighty Acts," *Spurgeon Sermons*, vol. 6 (London: Funk & Wagnalls Company, 1900).

124   "John Wesley," Wikipedia, last modified March 31, 2022, https://en.wikipedia.org/wiki/John_Wesley.

125   Wiersbe, *50 People Every Christian*.

126   Elizabeth Elliot, "Elizabeth Elliot Quotes."

127   Davids, *NIGTC: The Epistle of James*.

128   Allen, ed. *The Broadman Bible Commentary*.

129   Allen, ed. *The Broadman Bible Commentary*.

130   Allen, ed. *The Broadman Bible Commentary*.

131   Christianity, "Timeline: Spurgeon's Service at Surrey Gardens." Last updated July, 2007, https://www.christianity.com/church/church-history/timeline/1801-1900/spurgeons-service-at-surrey-gardens-11630503.html.

132   Charles H. Spurgeon, "A Psalm of Remembrance," *Spurgeon Sermons*, vol. 6 (London: Funk & Wagnalls Company, 1900).

133   Beth Moore, "Beth Moore Quotes," AZ Quotes, accessed April 3, 2022, https://www.azquotes.com/author/10320-Beth_Moore.

134   John Piper, "How to Know the Will of God: Finding Direction with the Renewed Mind," Desiring God, accessed September 27, 2021, https://www.desiringgod.org/messages/how-to-know-the-will-of-god.

135   Andrew Boryga, "Man Dives in to Save Unconscious Woman in Sinking Car," *South Florida Sun Sentinel*, accessed September 29, 2021, https://www.sun-sentinel.com/local/palm-beach/fl-ne-car-canal-rescue-sunday-20200224-a7thhnnbzvcivjji-aapnbfakte-story.html.

136   Allen, ed., *The Broadman Bible Commentary*.

137   Nwamaka Onyekachi, "21 Inspiring Quotes that Can Move You to Return to God," Heart Rays: Inspiration, Love, Life, Style, May 12, 2017, http://www.amakamedia.com/2017/05/21-inspiring-quotes-that-can-move-you.html.